EMPIRE OF ANCIENT GREECE

REVISED EDITION

GREAT EMPIRES OF THE PAST

EMPIRE OF ANCIENT GREECE

REVISED EDITION

JEAN KINNEY WILLIAMS

JOHN W. I. LEE, HISTORICAL CONSULTANT

CHELSEA HOUSE
PUBLISHERS
An imprint of Infobase Publishing

Great Empires of the Past: Empire of Ancient Greece

Chelsea House
An imprint of Infobase Publishing
132 West 31st Street
New York NY 10001

Library of Congress Cataloging-in-Publication Data
Williams, Jean Kinney.
Empire of ancient Greece / Jean Kinney Williams.—Rev. ed.
    p. cm.—(Great empires of the past)
Includes bibliographical references and index.
ISBN 978-1-60413-165-9
1. Greece—History—To 146 B.C.—Juvenile literature. 2.
Greece—Civilization—To 146 B.C.—Juvenile literature. I. Title. II.
Series.

DF215.W58 2009
938—dc22   2009004460

Chelsea House books are available at special discounts when purchased in bulk quantities for businesses, associations, institutions, or sales promotions. Please call our Special Sales Department in New York at (212) 967-8800 or (800) 322-8755.

You can find Chelsea House on the World Wide Web at http://www.chelseahouse.com

Produced by the Shoreline Publishing Group LLC
Editorial Director: James Buckley Jr.
Series Editor: Beth Adelman
Text design by Annie O'Donnell
Cover design by Alicia Post

Printed in the United States of America

Bang MSRF 10 9 8 7 6 5 4 3 2 1

This book is printed on acid-free paper.

CONTENTS

INTRODUCTION

THE TERM *ANCIENT GREEKS* CAN REFER TO MANY CULTURES and times in world history. The ancient Greeks include the warriors who fought in the Trojan War in the 1200s B.C.E. and whose mythical stories, retold by Homer, are considered the foundation of Western literature. They also are the sophisticated (from the Greek word *sophos*, which means "wise") Athenians of what is known as Classical Greece. They gave us democracy in the 400s B.C.E. and their architecture and literature still influences modern society. And they are the Mediterranean peoples who, in the two centuries before Rome began its rule of the Western and Near Eastern world in the 140s B.C.E., made groundbreaking contributions to science and mathematics.

The history of the ancient Greeks spanned many centuries, from about 1600 B.C.E. to 146 B.C.E. As their world was unfolding, their Mediterranean neighbors included Egypt, whose civilization had already existed for 2,000 years. To the east, in modern-day Turkey, the Hittites made up another powerful kingdom that battled with Egypt for control over Syria, which lay between them. The nearby Phoenicians first developed an alphabet and advanced the art of shipbuilding. Trade and exchanges of culture and technology flourished among these kingdoms around the Mediterranean Sea. Eventually, the early Greeks became another important force in the area.

Ancient Greece was never a unified country. Rather, it was a collection of perhaps as many as 1,500 independent city-states (cities that function as separate nations). The people of those city-states shared a culture and a language, even though they were scattered throughout the modern-day Greek mainland and also around the Mediterranean and

OPPOSITE
Even in ruins, the Parthenon, a temple honoring Athena, the patron goddess of Athens, shows the beauty and power of Classical Greek culture. When it was built, the Parthenon was 101.34 feet wide and 228.14 feet long. It was made of brilliant white marble, had 46 supporting columns, and contained a statue of Athena that was nearly 40 feet tall.

CONNECTIONS

What Are Connections?

Throughout this book, and all the books in the Great Empires of the Past series, there are Connections boxes. They point out ideas, inventions, art, food, customs, and more from this empire that are still part of the world today. Nations and cultures in remote history can seem far away from the present day, but these connections demonstrate how our everyday lives have been shaped by the peoples of the past.

Black Seas (including today's Turkey, North Africa, and southern Italy). As the Greek philosopher Plato described, they sat like frogs around a pond. (ca. 429–ca. 347 B.C.E.).

These people did not call themselves Greeks, either. That name comes from the Romans, who called them *Graeci*. The Greeks always referred to themselves, and still do, as *Hellenes*. *Hellas* was their word for the entire Greek world, and is what Greeks today call their nation.

The image that most likely comes to mind when thinking about the "ancient Greeks" is that of Athens in the fifth century B.C.E.—what today is known as Classical Greece. Perhaps it is a scene from the crowded agora, or marketplace, bustling with vendors and shoppers. Or philosophers such as Socrates (ca. 470–399 B.C.E.), who drew crowds around them as they discussed their ideas about how to live a virtuous life. Or perhaps the Parthenon, the architectural masterpiece of its day. Or graceful statues of the gods and goddesses featured in Greek mythology, and the stories about them that are still told today.

All of those impressions come from the era during which the Greeks had enormous influences in their Mediterranean world, under the leadership of their largest city-state, Athens. Classical Greece should also come to mind during election campaigns, because the idea of democracy was invented by the ancient Greeks.

THE EARLIEST GREEKS

The large island of Crete, south of Greece, was home to the Minoans (who did not speak Greek). They were the first kingdom in the Aegean Sea (a part of the Mediterranean Sea that lies between modern-day Greece and Turkey). By about 2000 B.C.E., Minoans were building elaborate palaces that had running water and drainage in most rooms. They had a highly developed society with a complex religion.

The Minoan culture eventually overlapped with the more aggressive Mycenaeans. Historians named this culture for the city of Mycenae on southern Greece's Peloponnese Peninsula. They consider the Mycenaeans to be the first ancient Greeks, and are connected to the future Greek civilization by language and religion. The Mycenaean era lasted roughly from 1600 to 1200 B.C.E., and it gave the Greeks the glorious legends of King Agamemnon and Achilles fighting at Troy, and of Odysseus traveling home from the Trojan War. The Mycenaeans, it is believed, eventually took over the Minoan kingdom, and Crete later became part of the Greek Empire.

During the 12th century B.C.E., invasions disrupted the Mediterranean region. It is not known exactly what or who caused the disruption of the Mycenaean civilization. There is a gap of several hundred years in the history of the entire Mediterranean region about which very little is known—a time some historians have referred to as a Dark Age. But by the mid-eighth century B.C.E., the descendants of the Mycenaeans had begun forming city-states around the Aegean Sea. They were sending out emigrants (people who leave their country to settle someplace else). These people spread the Mycenaean language and culture by creating new colonies around the Mediterranean.

GEOGRAPHY PREVENTS UNIFICATION

The Greeks never had a unified state with a single capital. Their geography certainly did not encourage it. Greece is a land of mountains, and the mainland is separated south from north by water, except for a narrow strip of land, called an isthmus, near the city of Corinth. Many of the mainland's city-states hugged the coastline and could only be reached by sea, since land travel was difficult and there are no rivers in Greece that can be safely traveled by boat.

Many Greeks also lived on the islands dotting the country's coasts. Each settlement therefore grew into an independent city-state with its own calendar, coins, laws, and government. They were united by a common language and religion, but they were politically divided.

The Greeks were also bound together by a shared culture. This included the stories of their favorite heroes and of the gods and goddesses who they hoped would make good things happen in their lives. In 776 B.C.E., the first all-Greek athletics competition was held in honor of their chief god, Zeus. In an event that symbolized their sense of unity, Greek men came together from all their cities and colonies. They gathered in Olympia in northern Greece to compete in races, wrestling, and other athletic events. The Greeks continued to hold Olympic Games every four years for 1,000 years.

As another result of their geographical location, the Greeks became expert seafarers. Their comfort at sea, coupled with the sophisticated economies of their Mediterranean neighbors, led them to go abroad frequently as traders and as mercenaries (foreign soldiers hired to fight for another country).

ATHENS AND SPARTA BECOME THE MAIN GREEK POWERS

By about 600 B.C.E., Sparta and Athens had emerged as the dominant Greek city-states. Sparta was on the Peloponnese Peninsula and Athens was in the region northeast of Sparta known as Attica. Corinth and Thebes also were significant powers.

The eighth, seventh, and sixth centuries B.C.E. are an era classified by historians as Archaic Greece (*archaic* is a word that means "very old"). This is when Homer's epic stories about the Trojan War and its aftermath, the *Iliad* and the *Odyssey*, were written down. (An epic is a long poem about the actions and adventures of heroic or legendary figures or about the history of a nation.) Historians are not sure if Homer's stories are true, but the Greeks considered these epics to be their own ancient history.

During the Archaic Period another writer, Hesiod, wrote down the oral legends about Greek gods in a book called *Theogony*. The exact birth and death dates of Homer and Hesiod are not known. In fact, Homer's actual existence is not even certain. Hesiod was active in the eighth century B.C.E., and the origins of works said to be written by Homer have also been traced to that period.

Starting in the sixth century B.C.E. philosopher-scientists were no longer satisfied with the explanation that the gods had arranged everything. They began to ask questions about the universe. Governments ruled by oligarchies (councils of aristocrats) were being developed among city-states. By the end of the sixth century B.C.E. there were no kings or emperors in ancient Greece. The one exception was Sparta. Following a long tradition, it had two kings. But their power was limited.

Plots of the *Iliad* and the *Odyssey*

The *Iliad* and the *Odyssey* are fictional epics that reflect Greek beliefs about their heroic past. The central plot of the *Iliad*—a war between the Trojans and the Greeks—is probably based on real events, but the *Odyssey* is pure fiction. Both stories have become classics of Western literature, and the characters and events in them have turned up in a wide variety of books, plays, poems, and movies through the ages.

The 10-year war in the *Iliad* begins when Paris, son of Trojan king Priam, is called upon to judge a beauty contest between the goddesses Aphrodite, Hera, and Athena. All three offer Paris bribes, but Aphrodite's bribe is the most tempting. She promises him the beautiful Helen—who is the wife of Menelaus, the Greek king.

Menelaus launches an expedition to recover his wife, Helen. He is assisted by the legendary warriors Achilles, Odysseus, Ajax, and Nestor. Menelaus's brother Agamemnon, king of Mycenae, goes with them as commander-in-chief of the expedition. The Trojan side is led by Hector, Paris's brother.

The story describes many conflicts within the ranks of the Trojans and the Greeks, including actions the gods disapprove of that cause the battle to tilt one way or another. Finally, the long war is ended when Achilles kills Hector.

The *Odyssey* is an account of Odysseus's trip home to Ithaca. It should have been a brief trip—just across the Aegean Sea and around the southern coast of Greece—but it ended up being a 10-year journey. Along the way, he and his men encounter an island inhabited by the Cyclopes, the one-eyed giant. They visit Hades, the underworld, and see their fallen friends from the Trojan War. They put wax in their ears as they sail past the beautiful but deadly singing of the Sirens, and farther on their ship has to sneak past a six-headed monster called the Hydra.

After more adventures, only Odysseus survives to return to Ithaca. He then has to reclaim his wife and kingship after a 20-year absence. While he was gone, many men pressured his wife, Penelope, to marry them, claiming Odysseus must be dead. But she put them off long enough to see the return of her husband. His legendary skill with bow and arrow clears his home of these would-be kings, and his family is reunited.

A storage jar called a krater shows scenes from the *Odyssey*, the famous epic poem by Homer that Greeks believed was part of their history.

What historians today call the Classical Greek era emerged in the fifth century B.C.E. and lasted through most of the fourth century B.C.E. In the 400s B.C.E., Athens truly became the heart of Classical Greece. It was a military and cultural leader among city-states, and it also put democracy into practice, which is government by the *demos*, the Greek word for "people." Athens used its mighty navy to establish an empire, taking control of many other city-states. Through this contact, some Athenian concepts of democracy spread around the region. Democracy took on its fullest form from 450 to 350 B.C.E.. beginning with Athenian leader Pericles (ca. 495–429 B.C.E.). During this period, all of Athens's male citizens participated in the government. Women and non-citizens (which included all foreigners and slaves), however, could not participate—a situation similar to the United States until the 20th century. Greek democracy lasted in stronger or weaker forms until the Roman Republic took over the Greek world in 146 B.C.E. Democracy did not appear again in the Western world for many more centuries.

The Greek city-states continually fought among themselves, but they came together to fight a powerful invader, the Persian Empire, first in 490 B.C.E. When the Persians returned 10 years later, the alliance of city-states that fought them off again was led by Athens. The Athenians felt the gods had shown them great favor by granting them victory. Their resulting pride and con-

CONNECTIONS

The First Marathon

When Persian troops landed at the Greek city of Marathon in 490 B.C.E., generals in Athens sent the Olympic runner Pheidippides to Sparta. His mission was to seek Sparta's help against the invaders. The Spartans, however, were holding religious ceremonies and could not send troops. When Pheidippides returned with the bad news, the Greek generals decided to attack anyway, and they won a major victory over the Persians.

Today's marathon foot race takes its name from that event in Greek history. The modern marathon is just over 26 miles, which is about the distance between Athens and Marathon. In the first modern Olympics, which were held in Athens in 1896, the winner of the marathon was a Greek man named Spiridon Louis.

During his famous run to Sparta, Pheidippides covered about 147 miles, and there is no historical record that he ran from Marathon to Athens. (In other versions of the ancient story, an unnamed runner, not Pheidippides, ran from Marathon to Athens after the battle to bring news of the Greek victory.) In 1983, a group of runners started a new event that covers the approximate route Pheidippides most likely took. They called the race the Spartathlon. Top runners have completed the course in less than 24 hours.

CONNECTIONS

Ancient Greek Words Used Today

Many words in the English language come from ancient Greek. The English word *physics*, for example, comes from the Greek word *physis*, which means "nature." The Greek word *atomos*, meaning "indivisible," led to the English word *atom*, which refers to the smallest particle of an element.

Greek words are also at the heart of many prefixes and suffixes used in English and other European languages. For example, the prefix *dino* for the word *dinosaur* comes from the Greek word *deinos*, which means "terrifying." The suffix comes from the Greek work *sauros*, which means "lizard."

fidence inspired them to begin an ambitious plan to beautify their city and extend their influence.

Although Athens and Sparta ruled different areas of the mainland, the rivalry between the two deepened as Athens's power and status increased. Sparta was unique among the Greek city-states because it had a social structure based on a purely military model. The two city-states had little in common when it came to politics or philosophy. Finally, they went to war with one another in 431 B.C.E. in a conflict now known as the Peloponnesian War.

MACEDONIAN AND ROMAN CONQUEST

The Peloponnesian War began between Athens and Sparta, but eventually involved almost all of Greece. When it finally ended in 404 B.C.E., Sparta was the winner and Athens was greatly weakened. Seventy years later, the Greeks were no match for a new superpower from the north, Macedon. Its ruler, Alexander III (also known as Alexander the Great, 356–323 B.C.E.), took control of all of Greece and then defeated the Persian Empire. In his continuing conquests, Alexander spread Classical Greek culture across a huge area in just a few years.

After Alexander's death, his top generals each took a piece of his empire. This included the Greek world, Northern Africa, and the Near East. They continued Greek cultural traditions by preserving and advancing the study of science, mathematics, philosophy, and history.

The Italian artist Raphael (1483–1520) painted "The School of Athens" on the wall of the Pope's Palace in the Vatican in about 1510. It shows a gathering of Greek philosophers in a fictional scene. In the center are Plato (on the left, in a red garment and holding his hand up) and Aristotle (on the right, in a light blue garment holding a book). Ancient Greek culture was greatly admired throughout history.

Greek became a widely spoken language in the Western and Near Eastern world. When the Romans conquered those same regions in the mid-second century B.C.E., they, too, learned from the Greeks and built upon what they learned.

When Rome finally fell eight centuries later, the classical culture of Greece and Rome was largely forgotten in the West. But the art, science, and culture of the Greeks were preserved in great libraries by the Islamic Empire. At a time when Western Europe had largely lost this knowledge, Islamic scholars expanded upon Greek scientific ideas. Classical ideas were rediscovered and brought alive again during the European Renaissance in the late 15th century C.E. Painting and sculpture (often with Classical Greek and Roman themes) and the serious study of science, architecture, literature, and philosophy all advanced again in Europe.

In the 18th century, a new republic that called itself the United States of America borrowed an idea from an ancient republic. The idea was government of, by, and for the people. Like Athens's original democracy, that of the United States was not without flaws. In its early form, only white male citizens who owned property could participate. Also, as in Athens, slavery was legal.

In fact, the Founding Fathers of the United States preferred a more Roman model of democracy—one that gave less power to citizens who were not rich. What they did borrow from Athens was the ideals of equality before the law, the participation of citizens in their own government, and freedom of speech. In the history of the world, there have been very few cultures where a playwright such as Aristophanes (ca. 450–ca. 386 B.C.E.) could publicly make fun of the leaders he disagreed with in his plays—and win a prize for it.

To study ancient Greece, one also has to examine its darker side. Slavery was universally accepted and meant a brutal life for many people. It was legal to abandon an unwanted baby; the baby would either die or be picked up by another person and raised as a slave. Women and children had few rights. War was frequent as the city-states battled for land. While Athens could boast of the individual rights its male citizens enjoyed, it did not extend these rights to the city-states that it ruled.

But what set the Greeks apart from other ancient peoples were the questions they asked of themselves: How should people live? Is justice important? What values are truly worth striving for? The Greeks loved beauty and

CONNECTIONS

Power to the *Demos*

Demos is the Greek word that may have the most importance to Americans today. The idea that political power belongs to the *demos*, the people, is at the heart of the U.S. democratic political system. The word *democracy* is made up of the Greek words *demos* and *kratos*, which means "power."

The American democratic system, however, is very different from the original democracy of Athens. For example, Athenian citizens all gathered in one place to make decisions, and U.S. voters do not. Instead, Americans rely on elected representatives to carry out their wishes. This system was developed in ancient Rome, but was based on a Greek ideal.

Demos also appears as the root of several English words. *Demography,* for example, means recording and studying statistics about the population in a given area, focusing on such things as age, ethnic background, education, religion, and job status. (The word also has a Greek suffix—*graphy* comes from the Greek word *graphein*, meaning "to write.")

encouraged genuine intellectual and emotional expression. The theme of all works of Classical Greek art, science, mythology, philosophy, drama, and literature can be summed up in one phrase from the great philosopher Socrates: "Know thyself" (quoted in *Bartlett's Familiar Quotations*).

It is not an exaggeration to say that Western civilization today is built upon Classical Greek civilization. The Greeks left many cultural riches, from logic (the study of the rules and tests of sound reasoning) to democracy to rhetoric (the art of speaking or writing effectively) to drama to philosophy. What emerged from their many different city-states was a culture that set the foundation for our intellectual lives today. It is why students today still have much to learn from the ancient Greeks.

PART · I

HISTORY

THE BEGINNINGS OF CLASSICAL GREECE

THE ATHENIAN EMPIRE

THE FINAL YEARS OF CLASSICAL GREECE

CHAPTER 1

THE BEGINNINGS OF CLASSICAL GREECE

HISTORIANS CONSIDER THE EARLIEST EVIDENCE OF GREEK culture to be from a group that is now known as the Mycenaeans. They are called that because archaeologists first found artifacts (items from daily life that are left behind) belonging to them near the ancient town of Mycenae on the Peloponnese Peninsula. Like the Classical Greeks who came after them, the Mycenaeans lived in independent kingdom-communities but shared a common language and culture.

The Mycenaean civilization began about 1600 B.C.E., although it is not clear just how it originated. Their language was Indo-European, which means it shares its roots with languages from both Europe and India. Whether the Mycenaeans settled in Greece thousands of years before their written history began, or whether they conquered people already there in about 2000 B.C.E., is not known for sure. But they are connected to the later Greeks by language and religion.

The Mycenaeans were influenced by their neighbors, the Minoans. The Minoans lived on the large island of Crete, south of the Greek mainland and not far from the northern shores of Africa. The Minoans became wealthy by developing very efficient agriculture and by trading with other Mediterranean peoples. Some of their arts and handicrafts were similar to those of the Mycenaeans.

Mycenaean chieftains or kings lived in heavily walled palaces. Excavated towns and palaces of the seemingly peaceful Minoans on Crete, by contrast, show no walls. A variety of bronze weapons and armor has been found at Mycenaean burial sites, along with leather helmets and shields, some bronze drinking cups, and even a bronze comb

OPPOSITE
Many of the sacred buildings at Delphi can be visited today, although they are in ruins. This is the Tholos temple, the gateway to Delphi. It was built in the early fourth century B.C.E.

This golden funeral mask is from the Mycenaean culture. The Mycenaeans were ancestors of the Greeks and contributed much to later Greek culture.

with gold teeth. Weapons do not seem to have been passed down from father to son. The fact that each soldier had new weapons shows that these ancient warriors had some wealth.

By the mid-14th century B.C.E., the Mycenaeans were the most powerful force on the Aegean Sea. Warfare was carried out on a rather small scale compared to the big armies of the Egyptians and the Hittites. But the aggressive Mycenaeans were successful in their corner of the Mediterranean world. Most likely, they overran and absorbed the Minoan society.

The kingdom of Troy, once located along the Aegean coast in today's Turkey, was destroyed about 1230 B.C.E. Homer wrote in the *Iliad* about one long war between Troy and the Greeks (actually, the Mycenaeans). But archaeologists think Troy probably endured several attacks over many years.

The Mycenaeans lived in densely populated towns in today's Greece and across the Aegean Sea in modern-day Turkey. Their towns had a more centralized government than the Greek city-states that appeared a few centuries later. Technically, everything the society produced belonged to the king. Local rulers then divided up the wealth as they saw fit. Large palaces were built for the Mycenaean kings—the one at Mycenae may have been the palace of the overall king. At the peak of their civilization in the 13th century B.C.E., the Mycenaeans traveled far and wide in their Mediterranean world.

TROUBLE BREAKS OUT

About 1200 B.C.E., trouble erupted all around the Mediterranean. Groups of people were on the move throughout the region, destroying entire cities as they went. Palaces and artwork were destroyed, mostly by fire. Historians do not agree about who these destructive people were. (In fact, in recent years their very existence has become a subject of debate.)

In Egyptian records from the court of Ramesses III is a description, dated from around 1182 B.C.E., of attacks from "sea peoples" (as noted in Thomas R. Martin's book, *Ancient Greece: From Prehistoric to Hellenistic Times*): "All at once the people were on the move, dispersed in war. . . . No land could repulse their attacks."

The attacks caused the end of the Hittite Empire, located in eastern Asia Minor (the Hittite capital city of Hattusas was about 110 miles east of modern-day Ankara in Turkey). The Egyptian Empire shrank back to the area along the Nile River. The Dark Age had begun.

Greek historians from the age of Classical Greece wrote that at about this time, a large group of the Dorian people from the north (the ancestors of the Spartans) moved onto the Peloponnese Peninsula. The Mycenaeans fled across the Aegean Sea to Ionia, or Asia Minor, to escape them. The Mycenaeans lost their palaces. During the following few centuries, all use of their record-keeping script ended, as did trade between regions.

Modern historians have always believed the ancient historians. But more recently it has been argued that there is no archaeological evidence to show a large, sudden invasion into Greece in that period. Historians have proposed many theories, including famine, disease, climate change, civil war, and peasant uprisings, to explain the collapse of Mycenaean civilization. Still, no one is sure exactly what happened.

The Dark Age peoples had no written language or native art traditions to replace those that had disappeared. Because people were on the move, food production around the Mediterranean world decreased. The population was greatly reduced.

CONNECTIONS

The Greek Alphabet

The Mycenaeans used a kind of shorthand script for record keeping that was somewhat similar to that of the Minoans. The Greeks, however, borrowed their alphabet from the Phoenicians between 800 and 750 B.C.E. They adapted the Phoenician alphabet, called *cuneiform*, to form the Greek alphabet. They also took a few of the Phoenician consonants and used them as vowels.

The letters of the Greek alphabet are still used today in Greece, even though some letters now have slightly different pronunciations. And our word *alphabet* comes from the first two letters in the Greek alphabet, *alpha* and *beta*.

Greek letters usually appear in the West today in scientific work. For example, the brain waves produced during sleep are called delta waves, while an active brain produces beta waves. Greek letters are also used in math. Omega, the last letter in the Greek alphabet, is written Ω and can be used in equations to refer to Ohms, a unit of electrical resistance, while Σ, sigma, stands for the sum of many variables in a math equation.

Except for a few small prosperous areas, poverty became widespread throughout the region. Only Athens, located high atop a rocky outcrop, seems to have escaped large-scale destruction.

THE BEGINNING OF ARCHAIC GREECE

Greek peoples spread out across the Aegean Sea to Asia Minor. Their population had already shrunk, and no written records exist from that time. But, through songs or stories told aloud, the Greeks held on to their legends about King Agamemnon, Odysseus and Achilles, and the gods who helped them defeat the Trojans. These stories were a semi-historical memory of what Greeks believed about their past. They gave the early Greeks, who were so scattered geographically, a sense of unity.

The Dark Age ended at about the same time as the Greeks developed the technology to make iron tools. This was important because the stronger tools improved agricultural output. Gradually, prosperity began to return.

Burial sites from the ninth century, or 800s B.C.E., show increasing signs of material wealth. One Greek woman's grave dating from about 850 B.C.E. contained gold jewelry with the same designs as jewelry from the Near East. This means the Greeks had resumed trading with the Near East.

In the eighth century B.C.E., cities began to appear again, as Greeks and others around the Mediterranean slowly recovered from the disorder of the previous centuries. Historians refer to the period of Greek history between the end of the Dark Age and the beginning of the Classical era of the 400s B.C.E. as the Archaic period. It lasted from about 750 to 500 B.C.E.

By the 700s B.C.E., one military event signaled the end of the Dark Age in many ways. A battle was fought on the large island of Euboea in the Aegean Sea between the city-states of Eretria and Chalkis. The two armies were fighting over rich farmland. The island-city of Miletus aided Eretria, while Samos was allied with Chalkis. Most of those fighting were soldiers who traveled on foot, not on horseback. Painted pottery from that time shows soldiers with helmets topped with crests, spears, and round shields.

The battle was a perfect example of the new era because it marked a big change from the older style of warfare, where the officers were aristocrats who fought on horseback or chariots (two-wheeled carts pulled by horses). The battle also reflected a scene that would be played out over and over among the Greeks in the next few hundred years: A Greek city-state's army of heavily armed foot soldiers fighting with allies against another Greek city-state over farmland.

IN THEIR OWN WORDS

Achilles' Armor

In this section of the *Illiad*, Achilles is mourning over the death of Patroclus, his best friend, who was killed in battle. He was also wearing Achilles' armor at the time, so now the great warrior has none. Achilles' mother, Thetis, is a sea nymph (a mythical spirit). To comfort her son, she has the god Hephaestus make him a new suit of armor. (The Myrmidons are the Thessalian people, who were led by Achilles.)

> She found her beloved son lying face
>   down,
> embracing Patroclus' body, sobbing,
>   wailing,
> and round him crowded troops of morn-
>   ing comrades.
> And the glistening goddess moved among
>   them now,
> seized Achilles' hand and urged him,
>   spoke his name:
> "My child, leave your friend to lie there
>   dead—
> we must, though it breaks our hearts . . .
> But here, Achilles, accept this glorious
>   armor, look,
> a gift from the god of fire—burnished
>   bright, finer
> than any mortal has ever borne across
>   his back!"

> Urging, the goddess laid the armor down
>   at Achilles' feet
> and the gear clashed out in all its bla-
>   zoned glory.
> A tremor ran through all the Myrmidon
>   ranks—none dared
> to look straight at the glare, each fighter
>   shrank away.
> Not Achilles. The more he gazed, the
>   deeper his anger went,
> his eyes flashing under his eyelids, fierce
>   as fire—
> exulting, holding the god's shining gift in
>   his hands.
> And once he'd thrilled his heart with look-
>   ing hard
> at the armor's well-wrought beauty
> he turned to his mother, winged words
>   flying:
> "Mother—armor sent by the god—you're
>   right,
> only important gods could forge such work,
>   not many on earth could ever bring it off!
>   Now, by heaven, I'll arm and go to
>   war."

(Source: Homer, *The Illiad*, Translated by Robert Fagles, New York: Penguin Group, 1990.)

The remains of the site of the ancient Olympic games still stand in Olympia in Greece.

During this time, Homer's epic poems, the *Iliad* and the *Odyssey*, were written down in their present form. They had been preserved through an oral tradition—telling the story for an audience—for generations. These stories gave all Greeks, whatever their city-state, a proud past of heroes and gods. They also gave Western civilization its earliest literature.

Another important writer from that time was Hesiod. His work *Theogony* told the Greeks that their history went back to the beginnings of the universe and gave them detailed information about their gods. Some elements of those myths might have come from people who moved to the area during the Dark Age. But mostly, they were the old Mycenaean legends. Temples dedicated to the Greek gods were built at Delphi and Olympia in northern Greece and on the island of Delos. At Olympia, a temple was dedicated to Zeus, who was known as the father of gods and men. It was here that the first athletic contests were held in Zeus's honor—the Olympic games. The first games are believed to have been held in 776 B.C.E., and athletes from all over Greece attended. The games held at Olympia were a clear indication that even though the Greeks were scattered geographically, they maintained a common identity.

STARTING NEW COLONIES

As people became more settled and prosperity slowly returned, the Greeks began to send people out to form colonies. (A colony is an area that is under the political control of another country and is occupied by settlers from that country.) Mainland Greece is about 75 percent mountains. While olive trees and grapes grow successfully in Greece's thin soil, it has few good areas for growing grains such as wheat and corn. As a city-state's population outgrew its arable (farmable) land, colonization was one solution to the potential problem of food shortages.

The first colonists were sent to Cumae in southern Italy in about 750 B.C.E. Corinth's colony at Syracuse on the island of Sicily was established in 734 B.C.E., and would eventually become as significant as Corinth itself. Within 200 years, hundreds of Greek city-states and their colonies were in place from the western end of the Mediterranean Sea in modern-day Italy, France, and Spain, to the eastern end on the island of Cyprus. There were Greek settlements on Africa's north coast, around the Black Sea, and in Asia Minor.

By sending out colonies, overpopulation on the mainland was relieved, additional markets for Greek goods were created, and new Greek ports were established for all the trading that occurred around the Mediterranean. Sometimes colonists went willingly, sometimes they did not.

Some colonies were founded peacefully, and wives were easily found among neighboring populations. But sometimes it was more challenging. Land had to be fought for and wives perhaps kidnapped from among the area's natives. And sometimes a colony no longer wanted a connection with the mother city. The island colony of Corcyra (modern Corfu), for example, often had a rebellious relationship with its founding city-state, Corinth.

Before any group of colonists was sent out, the gods were consulted to make sure this was the right decision. Most often, Apollo's advice was sought at Delphi, where the gods were believed to speak through priestesses, sometimes called oracles.

Sparta and Athens established relatively few colonies. Instead, they conquered the land around them. Sparta conquered a southern area of the Peloponnese called Laconia and enslaved the neighboring people of Messenia. Athens grew into the large urban center of Attica by taking over all the surrounding land. Sparta's only colony, in Italy, was formed to send away a large group of illegitimate males (boys born to women whose husbands were away at war).

Rounding Up Colonists

In about 630 B.C.E., the residents of Thera, an island city-state, started the colony of Cyrene in what is today Libya in northern Africa. Thera had gone through several years of drought and could no longer support its population. According to an inscription found in Thera, the god Apollo, who was consulted through the oracle at Delphi, declared that it was necessary for people to leave and form the colony.

The inscription makes it clear that leaving one's hometown was not always voluntary. Any man from Thera who was chosen to leave faced death, the inscription read, if he did not cooperate. Anyone caught hiding a chosen colonist also faced the death penalty. If, after five years, the move proved to be too difficult, colonists could return home. But the colony's efforts were fruitful and Cyrene became an important source of grain for the Greeks.

CITY-STATES AND THEIR RULERS

The old villages and towns of the Mycenean era and the Dark Age began to develop into Greek city-states in the eighth century B.C.E. A typical city-state had an urban core, then spread out to include as much of the surrounding farmland as the city-state could control. Most city-states eventually bumped up against the outer boundaries of another city-state.

As the Dark Age passed, the city-states' kings gave way to councils of rulers from the cities' wealthier families. This form of government is called *oligarchy*, and it was unusual among the ancient civilizations. Sparta was a major exception, and had two kings.

Athens was among the oldest of the *poleis*, the plural of the Greek word for city-state. It is thought that sometime in the 700s B.C.E., several villages combined to form Athens, which is a few miles from a good seaport, Piraeus. Originally, all of Athens was on a high, flat hilltop—an easy spot to defend. But, like other city-states, as the population grew so did the city. Athens spread out around its hilltop, called Acropolis. The very top of the Acropolis became the location for its religious buildings.

As an important trade center, Athens came to control Attica, a narrow peninsula (50 miles across at the widest point) north of the Peloponnese Peninsula. Attica, with Athens as its urban core, was in the right spot for success. To its north were protective mountains, and its other sides were bounded by water (except for a thin strip of land at Corinth). Because Athens was close to the sea, it became a major trade center and also a starting and receiving point for new ideas and cultural exchanges.

Other significant city-states to emerge included Corinth, which was the commercial center of Greece in the 600s B.C.E. Corinth had two good ports, and its fine pottery was much in demand around the Mediterranean. Thebes became a large city-state in the lush farmlands of Boeotia, the region north of Attica. Inland Sparta conquered the lower half of the Peloponnese Peninsula and was also a powerful city-state.

Many Greek city-states shared a number of common traits, often based on their size. But Sparta stood apart in its form of government and its social structure. Many of its customs and practices seem shocking to modern people. But in its day it was a powerhouse that inspired fear and also admiration because of its devotion to discipline.

Sparta was formed when a few smaller villages combined to make a city-state. In two long wars during the eighth and seventh centuries B.C.E., ending in 630 B.C.E., this new city-state conquered and enslaved the people of a large area of the southern Peloponnese called

Messenia. The Spartans made Messenians serfs—agricultural workers who must work for a particular master, who owns the land. These former neighbors-turned-serfs were known as helots—a class of people who were not quite slaves but also were not citizens. The helots actually outnumbered the citizens of Sparta, and they always looked for opportunities to revolt. In response, Sparta became a strictly military society, primarily to keep watch over the large helot population.

CONNECTIONS

Welcome to the Polis

The Greek word for a city-state is *polis*. This is where we get the English words *politics* and *metropolis*, and modern city names such as Minneapolis and Indianapolis. *Pol* is used as a suffix for foreign cities too, such as Sebastopol in Russia. Polis is also the source of such words as *police* and *polity*, which means a political organization.

THE TYRANTS

By the 500s B.C.E., colonization had slowed because much of the available land around the Mediterranean region had been claimed. The populations of Greek city-states began to increase again, as did the number of working poor. Most Greek city-states granted citizenship to all their free-born males, but that did little to lift poorer citizens out of poverty. Farmers awaiting their harvest might be forced to borrow money or food that had to be repaid when their crops came in.

On the other end of the economic scale, the aristocracy, which owned the best or the most land (often both), was joined by a new class that grew rich from commerce. Some of these newly wealthy people, and some members of the aristocracy who genuinely believed the social system needed reform, seized the chance to take power.

These new leaders were called *tyrants*. Although today that word is used to describe a merciless ruler, it was not necessarily a negative label at first. The tyrants tried to give the people what they needed, because they needed support from the city's population—especially the new type of soldiers known as hoplites.

Except for Sparta, city-states did not have professional armies. All men from ages 18 to 60 (including foreigners living in the city) were expected to serve in the army whenever they were needed. The typical Greek hoplite was most likely a farmer who owned enough land—perhaps several acres that he worked alongside a couple of slaves—so that he could buy the necessary gear to be a soldier. Because the more successful Greek citizen-farmers were also soldiers and were essential for defense of their city-state, they had an increasingly powerful voice in the government. So, in a city-state such as Athens or Corinth, the successful tyrant was one who had support of the local hoplites.

In return for this support, a tyrant often helped the poorer classes by building large public works projects (often with wealth taken from the former rulers), such as city walls or new temples. These projects offered employment for many people. Sometimes the tyrants went a step further and reformed existing laws to make the justice system more balanced.

Athens was an exception. In Athens, if the harvest was bad in a particular year, poor land-owning peasants might be forced to sell themselves into slavery to pay their debts. While other city-states managed to find ways to balance the interests of the rich and poor, in Athens the rich refused to give up any of their wealth and power. Eventually, conflict between poorer classes demanding justice and the wealthy demanding payment led to threats of civil war. This, in turn, led to the most radical reform, Athenian democracy.

THE HOPLITES

The rise of tyrants in the bigger city-states came about at the same time the hoplites emerged. By the 600s B.C.E., hoplites were common

This ceramic container from about 500 B.C.E. shows a scene with hoplites. Hoplites were highly skilled, armored warriors. They were also part-time, volunteer soldiers, and therefore had some influence over public policy. If they were not satisfied with what their leaders did, they would not fight.

in city-state armies. The hoplite soldier was outfitted with a bronze helmet and breastplate, a broad, heavy shield, and an iron-tipped spear up to eight feet long. The shield had a distinctive double grip: The soldier put his whole arm through a band that ran across the center, and then held another small hand grip at the edge. This took all the weight off the wrist, and enabled him to hold up the heavy shield with one arm.

CONNECTIONS

The Spartan Tradition

Sparta had a rigidly structured society that was dedicated to warfare. The name of this Greek city-state led to the English word *spartan*, which has several meanings. It can refer to something that is plain and simple, rather than luxurious or fancy. People can be called spartan if they show tremendous self-discipline or deny themselves the finer things in life. High schools and colleges sometimes nickname their athletes the Spartans, reflecting the courage and skill Spartan warriors showed in battle.

Hoplites were extremely effective in battle. They marched in a very tight formation called a *phalanx*. Each soldier's shield overlapped the shield of the soldier next to him, leaving few places for enemy weapons to penetrate. The hoplites were difficult to stop as long as they stayed in their phalanx formation.

Altogether the hoplite carried and wore about 40 pounds of equipment in battle, which he paid for himself. The hoplite enjoyed a higher status than the traditional soldier, who perhaps had just a sword, or an archer who used a bow and arrows. Archers, for example, used their weapons from afar and avoided the close-up warfare the hoplites faced. Because less courage was required, the archers gained less status. Archers and other light-armed soldiers were also assumed to be of a lower economic class, since they could not afford the bronze hoplite armor.

In his book *The Wars of the Ancient Greeks*, author and classics scholar Victor Davis Hanson describes a likely encounter between two companies of hoplites, each representing a city-state or a confederation of city-states. The front rows of each company marched toward one another, each trying to remain in their phalanx while they broke up the formation of the other. Holding their 15-pound shields at chest height for protection, they used their spears against the enemy as the lines began to stumble or break apart. All of this was done under a blazing Mediterranean sun as the hoplites struggled in their bronze protective gear amid clouds of dust, with the bodies

The Phalanx

The poet Tyrtaeus wrote the first description of the phalanx in a piece about the Second Messenian War, which probably took place in the last third of the seventh century B.C.E. (The dates and details of Tyrtaeus's life are not clear. He seems to have been a Spartan, or at least to be living in Sparta.) Here, Tyrtaeus emphasizes how important it is to stay in formation.

> For those who, standing shoulder to shoulder, dare to come to close quarters and to fight among the foremost, fewer die and they preserve those behind them. All of the courage of cowards is dissipated. . . . Let each shake the mighty spear in his right hand and the frightening crest upon his head. Let each learn by practice to do the mighty deeds of war and not stand outside the range of the missiles with shield in hand. Rather everyone should close up to his man with his great spear or sword and wound or kill his enemy. Standing leg to leg, resting shield against shield, crest beside crest, and helmet to helmet having drawn near, let him fight his man with his sword or great spear.

Tyrtaeus obviously admired the courage of the hoplites who fight in the phalanx. He also said their courage in keeping in formation meant fewer of them are killed. But not everyone agreed. The Greek historian Herodotus (484–425 B.C.E.) attributed this passage to the Persian general Mardonius. In it, Mardonius criticized the way the Greeks fight in tight formations, out in the open. He said more of them die this way.

> Furthermore, I hear that the Greeks are accustomed to stirring up war in the most ill-advised way through their foolishness and stupidity. When they declare war on one another they find the best and flattest piece of land and go there and fight. The result is that the victors depart with heavy losses; about the losers I can't begin to say—they're utterly destroyed.

(Source: Tyrtaeus quoted in Sage, Michael M., *Warfare in Ancient Greece: A Sourcebook*. Florence, Ky.: Routledge, 1996; Herodotus quoted in Dewald, Carolyn, and John Marincola, *The Cambridge Companion to Herodotus*. Cambridge, U.K.: Cambridge University Press, 2006.)

of wounded and dead piling up around them. Greek city-states had frequent battles with one another over boundaries or other land control issues. A city-state did not hesitate to go to war to acquire more farmland if it would mean keeping the population fed. But although war was a common fact of life, large battles between Greeks in the Archaic period were unusual. Battles tended to be brief, perhaps lasting only an afternoon. This limited casualties and damage to the farmland they were defending or trying to acquire.

Strict discipline was the key to a successful hoplite army, and nobody practiced discipline better than the Spartans. Sparta, unlike all the other Greek city-states (1,500 of them), developed into an entirely military state in the Archaic period. Its professional hoplite soldiers were the most formidable in Greece. In fact, Spartan discipline was so tight that the system of government remained the same over many centuries. Rebellion against authority was considered un-Spartan.

ATHENS EXPANDS RIGHTS FOR POOR CITIZENS

In Athens, a coup (overthrow of the government) was attempted in 632 B.C.E. by a wealthy Olympic champion named Cylon. The attempt failed, but a decade later the ruling aristocrats squabbled among themselves and Athens seemed ready for another coup. Around 620 B.C.E., the aristocrats appointed Draco (dates unknown) to lead the city, with the hope that he would restore order.

Draco's rule in Athens was so harsh that even minor offenses could result in the death penalty. (His name is the root of our English word *draconian,* which means excessively harsh and severe laws.) Draco was also the first Athenian ruler to write down the laws in an official code, which meant the laws applied equally to all people, rich or poor. It also meant that after Draco's term as appointed ruler ended, his harsh laws remained in effect.

Under Draco's laws, rich landowners were able to take control of the property of any farmer who could not repay the money he borrowed for farming or food. More and more poor farmers in rural Attica outside Athens were set against wealthy landowners.

As suffering among the lower classes increased, civil war seemed a possibility. The ruling oligarchy chose Solon (ca. 630–ca. 560 B.C.E.) to be chief lawgiver in 594 B.C.E., with the authority to make reforms in the city's government. Solon was the logical choice for the position: He was born into the aristocratic class but was not personally wealthy. He was an intellectual and a poet.

He also sought a fairer balance between Athenian society's rich and poor. Solon restored to the poor control of land that had been taken in payment for debts. All peasants who had sold themselves into slavery for being in debt were freed. Use of the death penalty was primarily reserved for the crime of murder.

More importantly, any male citizen could use the courts to seek justice for a wrongdoing. The idea was born that political power for a broader range of male citizens and justice for all Athenian citizens should be part of the law. Although Solon was only in power for a year, he remained a deeply respected figure among Greeks in the centuries that followed.

But in spite of his improvements and a bustling economy, poverty was still widespread. Tension among the city's poor ran high. It was time for Athens's first tyrant.

Pisistratus (d. 527 B.C.E.) was a respected army commander who seized power in 560 B.C.E. His rule over Athens was firm by 546 B.C.E. Pisistratus left Solon's reforms in place, and further appealed to Athens's poor by starting public works projects to provide employment.

When Pisistratus died, his son Hippias (d. 490 B.C.E.) assumed leadership. Under Hippias, one of Athens's leading families, the Alcmaeonids, appealed to Sparta for help in removing him from office. The Spartans were glad to help. Then one of the Alcmaeonids, Cleisthenes (ca. 570–ca. 500 B.C.E.), assumed leadership of Athens.

Cleisthenes, who was from the same aristocratic family as Solon, firmly set Athens in the direction of democracy when he came to power in 508 B.C.E. He created an assembly of citizens with real power. This concept was unique in the ancient world. Many aristocrats believed it was dangerous to let the ordinary people have a voice in government.

Across the Aegean Sea, Ionian Greeks had more than inter-city squabbles or would-be tyrants to deal with. They had become subjects of the Lydian king, Croesus (d. ca. 546 B.C.E.). The newly-formed Persian Empire, founded in 550 B.C.E. by Cyrus the Elder (ca. 585–ca. 529 B.C.E.), defeated Croesus's army in 547 B.C.E. Anatolia and Ionia then became part of the Persian Empire.

In the next 25 years Cyrus added Egypt and Babylonia to his empire. He was followed by Darius I (r. 520–486 B.C.E.), who continued to expand the Persian Empire's boundaries, Darius got a few steps closer to mainland Greece when he defeated Thrace, a region northeast of Greece along the Aegean Sea. But the mainland of Greece remained independent.

Not long after the rule of Cleisthenes, however, Athens was faced with a challenge to provide leadership. The Persian Empire had finally set its sights on Greece. The independence of all the Greek city-states was now at stake.

CHAPTER 2

THE ATHENIAN EMPIRE

AT THE DAWN OF THE FIFTH CENTURY B.C.E., ATHENS WAS in position to become the leading city-state of Greece. Its seaport was always busy—a sign of its prosperity. Athens pulled ahead of Corinth, to the west, as the biggest trade center in the region. Foreigners (primarily people from other city-states) went to Athens to share in that success, even though they could not enjoy Athenian citizenship.

Major Athenian exports included olive oil produced from olives grown in the Attic countryside. The distinctive pottery of Athens, made from the local reddish-orange clay and decorated with black glaze, became a valuable export, and Athens overtook Corinth as the leading exporter of pottery. Slaves were also an important trading "product" in ancient commerce centers.

THE PERSIAN WARS

With mainland Greece free from foreign interference, Athens grew large enough to fight off attacks from Sparta, its primary rival. It continued its experiment with representative forms of government. This was a time when other Greek city-states were losing their independence. The island of Sicily, which was home to several city-states, endured many attacks from the Phoenician city-state of Carthage, located just across the Mediterranean in North Africa. To the east, Ionian Greek city-states came under the rule of the Lydians, until all of Anatolia fell to Persia's king Darius I. Darius's Persian Empire was centered in the Near East and stretched from Egypt to present-day Afghanistan.

OPPOSITE

The massive Acropolis still looms over the modern cityscape of Athens. The Acropolis was a huge temple complex. The Parthenon is part of this complex.

On this vase a Persian (left) and an Athenian warrior are shown in battle. The many Greek city-states united for the first time to defeat the invading Persians.

Athens became his target early in the fifth century B.C.E. Ionian Greeks rebelled against the Persian Empire in 499 B.C.E. Athens and Eretria sent military aid. Darius quickly regained control of Ionia, and now had a good excuse to invade mainland Greece and add it to his empire.

It appeared to be an easy task. The Greek world was very small compared to the Persian Empire. Although Darius sent only 20,000 to 30,000 soldiers—a relatively small force—it was still more than double the number of Greeks who eventually faced them. The Persian army arrived first at Eretria on the island of Euboea in 490 B.C.E. They burned the city-state as punishment for helping in the Ionian revolt.

From there, Marathon offered a good landing spot on the Greek mainland, because it was flat and was close to Athens. An Athenian army of 10,000 hoplites marched to the coast to meet the Persians. They were joined by 1,000 hoplites from the small city-state of Plataea. When the Persians appeared to be ready for battle, Athenian general Miltiades (ca. 554– ca. 489 B.C.E.) encouraged the Greeks to make the first move. The hoplites marched in phalanxes into the Persians' formation. Although they were greatly outnumbered, the Athenians maneuvered their troops to trap the Persians between a swamp and the sea. Their heavy armor protected them from Persian arrows and they fought with their long spears.

Expecting an attack on Athens to follow, the Greek army quickly marched more than 20 miles from Marathon back to Athens. But the Persians turned for home. The Greek historian Herodotus reported that the Persians lost 6,400 men, while the Athenians counted 192 dead and the Plataeans had even fewer. Although those figures may be exaggerated, they demonstrate the effectiveness of hoplite warfare.

Darius planned another attack, but he died in 486 B.C.E., leaving his son Xerxes (ca. 519–465 B.C.E.) to take revenge for the defeat. It took several more years for the Persian Empire to return. This time they brought 75,000 to 100,000 soldiers. However, the Persians faced a more united Greece. The Greek infantry, led by Spartan king Leonidas (d. 480 B.C.E.), numbered about 70,000 hoplites and about as many light-armed troops. As Xerxes' army made its way around the Aegean Sea in 480 B.C.E., the king correctly assumed that the smaller Greek city-states would surrender without a fight. The Greeks planned to meet the Persians with a big force in east-central Greece at a 50-foot-wide pass called Thermopylae.

Thermopylae was squeezed between cliffs and the sea. The Greek hoplites delayed the huge Persian army at this narrow pass for two days. Then a Greek traitor showed the Persians a little-known way around the pass and the Greeks were surprised from behind. Knowing they were now beaten, Leonidas and a force of slightly more than 300 hoplites, mostly Spartans, remained at Thermopylae to fight. Their plan was to delay the Persians while the rest of the Greek army retreated to defend the city-states to the south. Leonidas and his men were greatly outnumbered and had no hope of winning the battle. But if they could delay the Persians long enough, their main force could move into a better position to protect the rest of Greece. These brave Spartans, including Leonidas, fought until the last man was dead. They have an honored place in Greek legend and military history for continuing to delay an army many times their number.

The Athenians expected an attack and abandoned their city. The Persians then destroyed it—even the temples atop the Acropolis. Then another narrow pass, this time at sea, led to the Persians' defeat. Athens had the advantage because they had a large fleet of warships. Just before the Persians' second trip to Athens in 480 B.C.E., a rich deposit of silver had been discovered at Laurium in southern Attica. The Athenians used this wealth to build a fleet of several hundred *triremes*.

The Athenian warship, the *trireme*, was developed about the same time the hoplite soldier became common, around 600 B.C.E. It was most likely based on ship designs of the Phoenicians, who were expert sailors. The boat was long and narrow so it could move quickly and was easy to maneuver. The ships weighed up to 2,200 pounds and were powered by 170 oarsmen arranged in three rows, which is how the ship got its name—*treis* is Greek for "three." The oarsmen rowed together,

300 Spartans

The popular 2007 movie *The 300* retells the story of the Battle of Thermopylae. The film relates the main story, but adds many fantasy and magical characters. Despite this, some historians agreed that the basic facts of the film were surprisingly close to Herodotus's account of the battle. That was especially true of the heroic military attitudes of the Spartans. The movie starred Gerard Butler as Leonidas and was directed by Zack Snyder.

This plaster cast shows a team of oarsmen working in a Greek *trireme*—a ship with three rows of oarsmen. Greek ships were fast and easy to maneuver, and the Greeks were excellent sailors.

using the beat of a gong or a drum to keep the rhythm. The oarsmen rowed at a speed of up to 18 beats per minute.

The *trireme* had a ramming "beak"—a battering ram made of oak and reinforced with a bronze cap that stuck out from the bow at water level. (A battering ram is a heavy object swung or rammed against something to break it down.) The rowers sent the *trireme* into an enemy ship, making a hole in the hull.

At the time the *trireme* was developed, the Greeks fought primarily on land and naval warfare was rare. But 100 years later, it saved their civilization.

Under the leadership of Themosticles (ca. 524–459 B.C.E.), the Athenian fleet faced 400 to 500 Persian ships off the Greek coast just north of Athens. The *triremes* proved to be the better ships and much of Xerxes' fleet was destroyed. The Persian ships then turned around, leaving a still-large army behind in Boeotia. The Spartans led a successful defense effort there at Plataea, while Athens continued to chase the Persian fleet. The Persians were forced home. Once again, they were defeated by an enemy they greatly underestimated.

The key to this military victory was Greek unity. When they were faced with the threat of being ruled by a foreign power, 31 independent Greek city-states came together to fight a common enemy. It was the first time in their history that they acted as a united group.

Even more remarkable was the cooperation between Athens and Sparta, each of which normally viewed the other as an enemy. Athens and Sparta continued their alliance long enough to drive out the remaining Persians from Ionia, Anatolia, and northern Greece.

Athenian leaders were now convinced of the effectiveness of *trireme* warfare. They proposed forming and leading a league of city-states to build an even stronger navy, because everyone in Greece assumed the Persians would eventually return. The Greek historian Thucydides (d. ca. 401 B.C.E.) wrote in his *History of the Peloponnesian War* that the leaders of Sparta were glad to let the Athenians take on that responsibility.

The naval alliance was organized and dominated by Athens. It consisted of the city-states that were most in danger of Persian attack: those in Ionia and on the islands in the Aegean Sea. Larger city-states contributed *triremes* and their crews, while smaller ones combined their resources to provide wealth or one ship. The alliance was called the Delian League, because the money was kept at the temple of Apollo on the island of Delos. (City and other treasuries often were kept at a temple where, it was believed, the god would protect them.)

The Parthenon

After the Persians destroyed the religious buildings atop the Acropolis, Athenians allowed the rubble to remain as a reminder of what they had suffered and how they had defeated a powerful foe. But as the second half of the century began, Pericles began rebuilding the Acropolis. A new temple to Athena was planned to replace the first temple to Athena, Athena Polias ("guardian of the city"). The Parthenon ("house of the virgin goddess") was much grander in size, design, and decoration and was under construction for 15 years.

Pericles' enemies complained about how expensive the project was. But it employed builders, artists, and other craftsmen—helping to maintain Pericles' political power. It also was a proud declaration of the special relationship the people of Athens believed they enjoyed with the goddess Athena, and of the greatness of Athens. By building the Parthenon, Athenians announced for all to see that Athena approved of her city's strength in defeating the Persian Empire.

FROM LEAGUE TO EMPIRE

Athens was a natural center for the Delian League. The city had shipyards to build *triremes* and it had a lot of urban poor people who needed jobs, such as rowing the ships. One *trireme* provided work for

The Cost of Greatness

In *The Wars of the Ancient Greeks*, Victor Davis Hanson offers figures on how much Athens had to spend to become an empire. To build, equip, and staff one *trireme* cost between 10,000 and 12,000 drachmas, with one drachma being a day's wage for the average working Athenian. Keeping 100 *triremes* afloat and manned for one month cost 1.4 million drachmas; at the height of the empire, Athens had as many as 300 *triremes* in its navy.

Compared to fighters on horseback, hoplites were a bargain, because a hoplite soldier spent his own money (about 200 drachmas) on his armor and equipment. The Athenian or Spartan government might expect to spend 70,000 drachmas to keep 10,000 hoplites in the field for one week. One good war horse, on the other hand, could cost several hundred or even thousands of drachmas.

At the outbreak of the Peloponnesian War, Athens and its allies had 400 *triremes*. Sparta had none and its allies had 100. Sparta, as usual, preferred to invest in hoplites. It commanded 40,000 as the war began, while Athens commanded 23,000.

170 lower-class paid oarsmen. In addition to rowers, each *trireme* carried about 30 soldiers—a few officers and the rest hoplites.

Over time, the other city-states in the Delian League mainly contributed money to the military effort. The treasury of the league was moved to Athens, which now had a lot of money to spend. Even though it eventually became clear that the Persians were not returning to Greece, military representatives were quick to visit any city-state that tried to pull out of the league. For example, when the island city-state of Thasos tried to withdraw, Athenian *triremes* arrived to enforce its membership.

By the 470s B.C.E., the Delian League had become an Athenian Empire. Athens had built and now commanded more than 300 *triremes*. It was very expensive to maintain such a large force. But Athens was taking in large amounts of money from its silver mines and from the league, which had more than 150 members at its peak.

Sparta's military might protected it from Athens. Sparta had formed its own alliance, the Peloponnesian League. The league kept peace on the Peloponnese Peninsula for more than a century. Nevertheless, the growing power of Athens was alarming to Sparta.

CLASSICAL ATHENS

By the middle of the fifth century B.C.E., Athens saw itself as the leading city-state in Greece. Most of its neighbors agreed. The aristocrat Pericles (495–429 B.C.E.) came to power in 458 B.C.E. as one of 10 generals elected by Athens's General Assembly to be both military and civil leaders. Under Pericles' guidance, the Athenian Empire reached its largest size. Athenian democracy, which first budded under Solon's rule, firmly established many individual rights that are still cherished today, including freedom of speech.

Pericles made peace with the Persian Empire and also negotiated a 30-year treaty with Sparta in the 440s B.C.E. There was always some small military action between Athens and its allies, or between Athens and Sparta's allies, such as Corinth. But there were no major wars in the mid-fifth century B.C.E. and Pericles was able to turn all his attention upon Athens. The large sums of money provided by the Delian League and the Laurium silver mines was used to maintain a strong navy, but Athens's big income also financed some democratic reforms. These included daily pay for men chosen to serve on a jury or in the assembly, as well as an extensive public building program.

As Athens's prosperity continued, people from other countries and city-states moved to the city to find work. Pericles was concerned that these new arrivals would soon have too much influence. So he narrowed the qualifications for citizenship; now, both parents had to be born in Athens for a person to be a citizen. That made it impossible to marry an Athenian and gain citizenship. Pericles also expanded trade to the Black Sea area, from which grain and fish were imported.

The Athenian navy employed tens of thousands of urban poor, and their support enabled Pericles to stay in power for nearly 20 years. Pericles and the democratic system had their enemies, though. Handing so much power over to the *demos* bothered many aristocrats, who did not trust the judgment of the ordinary people.

Yet, despite some conflict between the higher and lower classes, life in Athens in the mid-fifth century B.C.E. was good for most people. There was not a great economic divide between the rich and the poor. All male citizens were expected to participate in their own government. "Unlike any other community, we Athenians regard him who takes no part in these civic duties not as unambitious, but as useless," said Pericles in a speech recorded by Thucydides. "In short,

I say that as a city we are the school of all Hellas" (as quoted in *The Landmark Thucydides*).

ATHENS'S ANGRY NEIGHBORS

The Classical age of Athens was not good for slaves or the city-states that competed with Athens. Some city-states, such as Megara and Corinth, saw their trade ruined, or at least crowded out, by the expansion of Athens. Thebes, in the lush agricultural region of Boeotia, resented the power Athens held over its neighbors. Sparta to the south was becoming alarmed at Athens's growth and ambition.

Corinth and other city-states on the Peloponnese Peninsula were under the control of Sparta, while Athens controlled lower Attica, Macedon, and Thrace in northern Greece, the large island of Euboea, and the coastal city-states of Ionia. Much of the conflict between Sparta and Athens in the 430s B.C.E. was sparked by their tendency to get involved in the affairs of one another's allies. Sparta believed it needed to maintain strict control in order to continue dominating its large helot population. But Athens helped Corinth's colony, Corcyra, when it clashed with its mother city. Then one of Athens's unwilling allies, Potidaea, sought help from Corinth to rebel.

Pericles put Athens on a path to war by refusing to negotiate any of these issues with Sparta. Twenty years after Pericles came to power, Spartan leaders no longer felt they could tolerate Athens's unchecked growth. The 30-year treaty between Athens and Sparta was not even 15 years old, but war was at hand.

The Greeks had united to keep the Persian Empire from grabbing control of the mainland. Now they were about to fight each other in what would turn out to be much more than an afternoon battle over farmland. With the extensive system of allies each had developed—the Delian League and the Peloponnesian League—war between Athens and Sparta would mean war for much of Greece.

THE PELOPONNESIAN WAR

The Peloponnesian War began in 431 B.C.E., when Sparta attacked the Attica countryside. Although Athens faced a powerful enemy, it was surrounded by a sturdy wall that had been strengthened just after the Persian wars. Athens's port, Piraeus, was a few miles away and was also walled. So was the road between Piraeus and Athens.

The whole structure became known as "the long walls." The walled road meant no enemy could starve the city by surrounding it. Athens had access to food through shipments coming into its port. And Piraeus was protected by the strong Athenian navy.

The war was actually fought in phases. The first one lasted from 431 to 421 B.C.E. Five times during that period, Spartan forces attacked the Attica countryside, destroying crops. The rural residents took refuge within the already-crowded city of Athens. Spartan soldiers stayed for just a few weeks, because they were always afraid to leave their *helots* unguarded for too long. But in those few weeks they

IN THEIR OWN WORDS

Ready to Go

Greek historian Thucydides wrote *The History of the Peloponnesian War*. Thucydides was an Athenian officer. After he lost an important battle, he was sent away from Athens. He then spent time among the Spartans and their allies, and was therefore able to observe both sides during the war.

In this excerpt, he describes how much Sparta and her allies wanted to go to war against Athens.

And if both sides nourished the boldest hopes and put forth their utmost strength for the war, this was only natural. Zeal [enthusiasm] is always at its height at the commencement [beginning] of an undertaking; and on this particular occasion the Peloponnesus and Athens were both full of young men whose inexperience made them eager to take up arms, while the rest of Hellas stood straining with excitement at the conflict of

its leading cities. Everywhere predictions were being recited and oracles being chanted by such persons as collect them, and this not only in the contending cities. . . . Men's feeling inclined much more to the Spartans, especially as they proclaimed themselves the liberators of Hellas. No private or public effort that could help them in speech or action was omitted; each thinking that the cause suffered wherever he could not himself see to it. So general was the indignation felt against Athens, whether by those who wished to escape from her empire, or were apprehensive of being absorbed by it. Such were the preparations and such the feelings with which the contest opened.

(Source: Strassler, Robert B., editor, *The Landmark Thucydides: A Comprehensive Guide to the Peloponnesian War.* New York: The Free Press, 1996.)

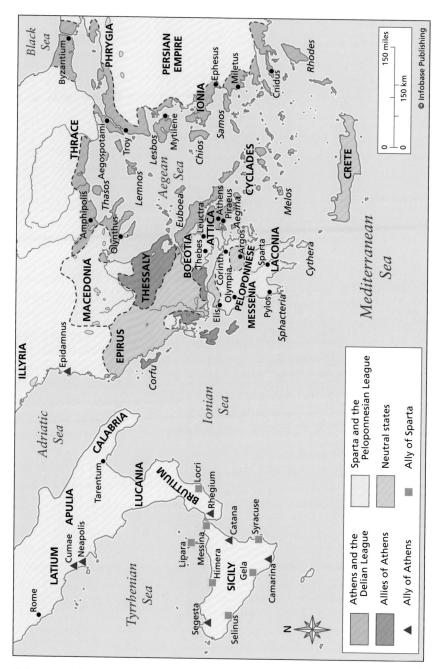

Athens and Sparta, and their many allies, squared off during the Peloponnesian War. This map, ca. 431–404 B.C.E., shows the loyalties of the many city-states and colonies in the Greek sphere of influence.

IN THEIR OWN WORDS

Honoring Fallen Soldiers

Pericles used his very effective oratorical, or public speaking, skills to inspire the Athenians. One of his most famous speeches was a funeral oration he gave honoring the Greek soldiers who died during the first phase of the Peloponnesian War. He also reminded the Greeks that more fighting lay ahead. The speech was recorded by Thucydides. After Pericles praised the accomplishments of long-dead ancestors, he said:

Our constitution does not copy the laws of neighboring states; we are rather a pattern to others than imitators ourselves. Its administration favors the many instead of the few; this is why it is called a democracy. . . . The freedom which we enjoy in our government extends also to our ordinary life. There, far from exercising a jealous surveillance over each other, we do not feel called upon to be angry with our neighbor for doing what he likes, or even to indulge in those injurious looks which cannot fail to be offensive, although they inflict no real harm.

For Athens alone of her contemporaries is found when tested to be greater than her reputation. . . . The admiration of the present and succeeding ages will be ours, since we have not left our power without witness, but have shown it by mighty proofs. . . . Such is the Athens for which these men , in the assertion of their resolve not to lose her, nobly fought and died; and well may every on of their survivors be ready to suffer in her cause.

Indeed if I have dwelt at some length upon the character of our country, it has been to show that our stake in the struggle is not the same as theirs who have no such blessings to lose. . . .

Modern historians believe this speech was an important influence for President Abraham Lincoln (1809–1865) when he wrote the Gettysburg Address—a speech he gave at the dedication of a Civil War cemetery. Like Pericles, Lincoln looked back to the past as he remembered the successful American Revolution and honored the dead in a current war. And, like Pericles, Lincoln talked of "unfinished work," since the war was not yet over.

(Source: Strassler, Robert B., editor, *The Landmark Thucydides: A Comprehensive Guide to the Peloponnesian War.* New York: The Free Press, 1996.)

seriously damaged the countryside. Their plan was to draw the Attica hoplite farmers out from behind Athens's walls for a fight.

Although Attica did not have very fertile farmland, it had well-established olive groves. The Spartan attacks destroyed olive crops that were ready for harvest, or sometimes the trees themselves. Olive trees

This is Alcibiades, an Athenian aristocrat and naval leader. During the Peloponnesian War, he switched sides and joined with Athens's enemy, Sparta. Then he switched sides again and lead a key naval victory over Sparta.

take at least 10 years to bear fruit, and several more years to reach their productive peak. Destroying so many trees seriously limited the ability of Attica's farmers to earn a living.

In addition, Athens was now seriously crowded with refugees. The conditions inside the walls of the city encouraged the spread of disease. By the second year of the war, plague swept through the packed streets. In 429 B.C.E., the plague killed Pericles himself, as well as many of the men who were needed to row the Athenian *triremes*.

Still, Athens did not send out its hoplites to fight those of Sparta and its ally, Thebes. Both of Athens's enemies had more and better armed infantry (soldiers who fight on foot). Instead, in 425 B.C.E., Athens had an important naval victory: Cleon (d. 422 B.C.E.), a prominent Athenian leader battle, captured the coastal Messinian city of Pylos and set large numbers of *helots* free. Athenian forces also captured nearly 300 Spartan hoplites, and told the Spartans they would all be killed if Sparta made any return visits to Attica. That kept Sparta out of Athenian territory for the remainder of this first phase of the war.

Athens suffered a significant loss the next year, when its hoplites finally ventured out against both Theban and Spartan forces at Delium. In one day's fighting, Athens lost more than 1,000 hoplites. Many of the Athenian survivors had to make a night-time run home, pursued by the enemy. Some of the Athenian hoplites (including the philosopher Socrates, whose bravery was remembered later by his pupil, Plato) continued to put up a fight as they were retreating.

In 422 B.C.E., both sides lost their top commanders in battle: Athens's Cleon and Sparta's Brasidas. After 10 years of fighting, Sparta had captured only a little territory in Attica and a temporary peace began in 421 B.C.E. But there was no real end to the war. Both city-states had leaders who only wanted to end the conflict when their enemy completely surrendered.

DISASTER IN SICILY

The years 415 to 413 B.C.E. were disastrous for Athens. At the center of the disaster was a young aristocratic politician named Alcibiades (450–404 B.C.E.). At one time, he had been a member of Pericles' household. Alcibiades was one of the survivors of the battle at Delium.

Alcibiades urged the Athenian Assembly to send a naval force to Syracuse. This city-state was one of Corinth's colonies, an ally of Sparta, and a rich and prosperous prize. Although Syracuse was 800 miles away and was well-defended, Alcibiades' arguments were tempting. So were Syracuse's riches.

The expedition was approved in 415 B.C.E., and Alcibiades was named to lead it. But on the day the ships set sail, dozens of statues of

---

The City Walls

The first wall around the city of Athens was built in the sixth century B.C.E. during the reign of Pisistratus (d. 527 B.C.E.). After the victory over the Persians, the walls were strengthened, supposedly with the help of all the city's men, women, and children. Most residents of the *polis* lived outside the city's walls.

Hermes were damaged. Hermes was the god with wings on his sandals who protected travelers and boundaries, among other duties. The damaged statues had been scattered throughout the city, placed at street intersections as well as on the ships ready to set sail. The very religious Greeks would not commit such an anti-religious act without much anger behind it. It was considered an extremely bad omen (a sign that predicts the future).

Alcibiades ordered the expedition to sail anyway. His enemies accused him of the serious crime of damaging the statues, and a ship was sent after him to bring him home to stand trial. Alcibiades then changed sides and joined Sparta. The remaining ships pushed on. But they suffered total defeat at Syracuse, which had its own navy. It also had help from the new Peloponnese fleet, which was funded by the Persian Empire. The famous Athenian fleet was destroyed and 40,000 Athenian men were killed or enslaved.

Athens was now at its weakest point since the war began. The Spartans stationed a number of troops year-round near the city-state's walls. With Athens's defenses spread so thin, 20,000 Athenian slaves, many of them working in the Laurium silver mines on the southern tip of Attica, saw an opportunity to escape. They fled to the Spartans. This cut Athens off from much-needed income. Working for the Spartans now, Alcibiades went to Ionia and stirred up rebellion against Athens among her allies.

A PEACE OFFER IS REJECTED

But Athens was not defeated yet. It had money set aside in the treasury at the Parthenon and drew on that to rebuild a fleet. It won some battles off the coast of Ionia. But within the city of Athens, a new problem arose: The ruling aristocrats were overthrown by a group of anti-democratic aristocrats who wanted to do away with the general assembly. Alcibiades was part of the plot, even though he was far away. He hoped that when power changed hands in Athens, he could return home.

When Athens's naval crews received news of the overthrow, they threatened to return home and restore the democratic government by force. A compromise council was formed. It offered to forgive any crimes against anyone who had been forced to leave. This included Alcibiades, who was still a highly-regarded military leader, even though he had betrayed Athens.

Alcibiades resumed his position as the head of a rebuilt Athenian navy and enjoyed a victory over Sparta on the southern coast of the Black Sea. According to another Greek historian, Xenophon (428–354 B.C.E.), the message sent home by a Spartan officer after that battle was typically spartan in its briefness: "Ships lost. Commander dead. Men starving. Do not know what to do" (as quoted by Thomas Martin in *Ancient Greece: From Prehistoric to Hellenistic Times*).

After losing the battle, Sparta offered peace. But Athens rejected the offer. The Athenians wanted not just peace, but to conquer Sparta. Sparta needed money to continue the war, and gave the Persians permission to retake western Anatolia in exchange for gold. Sparta's rebuilt navy defeated Athens in battle and blocked food shipments to the Athenian port of Piraeus. Athens finally surrendered in 404 B.C.E. Its days as a military power were over.

CHAPTER 3

THE FINAL YEARS OF CLASSICAL GREECE

AT THE END OF THE PELOPONNESIAN WAR, SPARTA TORE down Athens's long walls and declared Greece to be free from the Delian League. Corinth pressed Sparta to completely destroy Athens, but the Spartans wanted to be sure a weaker Athens still existed as a balance to Corinth's power.

The Spartans established a new government in Athens—a group of leaders who came to be called the Thirty Tyrants. This group of wealthy aristocrats ruled just eight months, but their rule was extremely harsh. For example, their members would execute Athenian citizens in order to grab their property. Soon, the city-state of Thebes, Athens's long-time enemy, expressed sympathy for the Athenians. Rather than see Thebes and Athens become allies, Sparta stood quietly by while Athenians overthrew the Thirty Tyrants in 403 B.C.E.

Athens went about restoring its democratic government. But the city-state did not have the wealth it had enjoyed a few decades earlier. Food was scarce and the city was more crowded than ever. There was no income from the silver mines after Sparta freed the mine slaves, and golden objects in the temples were melted down to pay war debts. The Athenian empire, after a glorious half-century, was finished.

Historian M. I. Finley wrote in *The Ancient Greeks* that the devastation of Athens in the Peloponnesian War was disastrous for all of Greece. That is because Athens was the one city that might have been able to unify the city-states and thus maintain peace. Perhaps that could have led to a genuine nation, instead of the collection of city-states whose days of independence were nearly over.

OPPOSITE

Greek philosopher and teacher Socrates steered philosophy toward a study of behavior and morals. He explored important issues with his students by asking them questions. This style of teaching is still used today, and is known as the Socratic method.

THE RISE OF PHILOSOPHY

Athens's days of making major contributions to world culture had not ended, even though its status as a world power was greatly diminished after the Peloponnesian War. Philosophy (from the Greek word *philosophia*, which means "love of wisdom") was a sixth-century B.C.E. innovation that began on Ionia. Philosophy means asking why and how the world exists, and what place humans have in it, rather than accepting the conventional explanation that the gods control the universe and the fate of humans.

By the fourth century B.C.E., Athens had become the international center for a number of philosophical movements. The most famous of the Greek philosophers—Socrates, Plato, and Aristotle (384–322 B.C.E.)—all offered new ideas and thought, and attracted many students. (Aristotle was not an Athenian citizen, but went to Athens at the age of 18 to study with Plato.)

Socrates is credited with having steered philosophy toward a study of behavior and morals. Socrates' devoted student, Plato, taught Aristotle, who was also greatly interested in natural science. Aristotle became the tutor of the young prince of Macedon, later known as Alexander the Great. When Alexander established a vast empire, the ideas of his teachers reached around the globe.

In the fourth century B.C.E., as Greek city-states weakened and the future seemed less certain, some philosophical movements began to stress personal wisdom and inner contentment as the ideal goal for individuals.

A Peloponnesian Peace—*Finally*

When the fighting of the Peloponnesian War ended, neither Athens nor Sparta ever recovered their former greatness. The fact that the two main powers in the region were weakened made it much easier for Philip of Macedon to conquer the Greeks 70 years later. For 2,000 more years, the Greeks would be subjects of other empires, until they finally won independence again in 1829.

But the story did not end there. In 1996, the mayors of Athens and Sparta made the end of the Peloponnesian War official with a ceremony at Sparta. As reported in a March 12, 1996 broadcast of *All Things Considered*, the two mayors issued a joint statement that said, "Today we express our grief for the devastating war between the two cities of Ancient Greece, and declare its end." Each ancient city-state represented qualities to admire—Sparta's dedication to discipline, Athens's defense of individual freedom. The mayor of Athens told reporters that if these qualities were combined today, they could make a real difference in the world.

IN THEIR OWN WORDS

Socrates on Virtue

Socrates was well known during his own time for his conversational skills and public teaching. But he wrote nothing. We must therefore depend on the writings of his students to learn about Socrates' ideas.

Socrates' main teaching method was to engage in a discussion with his students. He would ask a series of questions about an issue, and also answer the questions of the students involved. Generally, the points of view expressed between student and teacher were different. Socrates used his questions to lead his students to eventually realize their teacher was correct. This form of inquiry has come to be known as the Socratic method.

Socrates' pupil Plato wrote a number of these dialogues that he attributed to Socrates. In this one, Socrates and Meno discuss human virtue: whether or not it can be taught, whether it is shared by all human beings, and whether it is one quality or many.

Socrates: *When you say, Meno, that there is one virtue of a man, another of a woman, another of a child, and so on, does this apply only to virtue, or would you say the same of health, and size, and strength? Or is the nature of health always the same, whether in man or woman?*

Meno: *I should say that health is the same, be it in man and woman.*

Socrates: *And is not this true of size and strength? If a woman is strong, she will be strong by reasons of the same form and of the same strength subsisting in her which there is in the man. I mean to say that strength, as*

strength, whether of man or woman, is the same. Is there any difference?

Meno: *I think not.*

Socrates: *And will not virtue, as virtue, be the same, whether in a child or in a grownup person, in a woman or in a man?*

Meno: *I cannot help feeling, Socrates, that this case is different from the others.*

Socrates: *But why? Were you not saying that the virtue of a man was to order a state, and the virtue of a woman was to order a house?*

Meno: *I did say so.*

Socrates: *And can either house or state or anything be well ordered without temperance and without justice?*

Meno: *Certainly not. . . .*

Socrates: *Then both men and women, if they are to be good men and women, must have the same virtues of temperance and justice?*

Meno: *True.*

Socrates: *And can either a young man or an elder one be good, if they are intemperate and unjust?*

Meno: *They cannot. . . .*

Socrates: *Then all men are good in the same way, and by participation in the same virtues? . . . And they surely would not have been good in the same way, unless their virtue had been the same?*

Meno: *They would not.*

Socrates: *Then . . . the sameness of all virtue has been proven.*

(Source: Plato, *Meno*, Translated by Benjamin Jowett, New South Wales, Australia: ReadHowYouWant, 2006.)

The Cynics and the Stoics were two significant movements that approached the goal of self-fulfillment from different directions.

Diogenes (ca. 400–325 B.C.E.), founder of the Cynic movement, said virtue is the only true good, and that real virtue lies in self-control and independence. He encouraged people to throw aside social conventions, which he viewed as expressions of false feelings. A *cynic* today is someone who believes people's actions tend to be motivated by self-interest—one element of Diogenes' philosophy.

Diogenes is famous today because of a search he undertook. He supposedly walked through Athens during the day holding a lit lamp. The lamp, he said, was to help him find an honest man. Diogenes obviously did not need the lamp during the day, and he did really not think he would ever find a truly honest man. In reality, he was making a comment on the state of his society. Today, people refer to Diogenes and his lamp when they want to highlight the difficulty of learning the truth, or when they begin a search that seems to have no end.

Greek philosopher Diogenes, shown here in an Italian Renaissance sculpture, is famous for a search he undertook. He walked through Athens with a lamp, looking for just one honest man.

Zeno of Citium (ca. 335–ca. 263 B.C.E.) founded the Stoic school of philosophy in about 300 B.C.E. Stoics taught that true wisdom came from throwing off passions and practicing virtue, regardless of any anxiety that might result. Today, a *stoic* person is not affected by strong feelings and disregards personal comfort in order to achieve greater goals, such as wisdom and integrity.

The fifth-century B.C.E. Sophists were traveling teachers who, for a fee, gave lessons in how to use logic to win an argument. Today, the word *sophisticated* describes someone who is knowledgeable and clever.

CITY-STATES COMPETE FOR POWER

As Athenian philosophers thought about virtue and justice, the Greek world was still finding reasons to make war—although that warfare was changing. Athens, Sparta, and Thebes spent the next 60 years vying for the position of top polis, often switching alliances. Athens and Sparta had to make do with fewer farmer-citizens filling the hoplite ranks and more mercenary soldiers and armed slaves.

Athens had to increase taxes to finance the ongoing wars, and Athenian farmers were finding it harder to sell their produce because other trading partners, such as Syracuse, had their own economies disrupted by war and invasions. More people then left their farms to join the armies as full-time professional soldiers.

In fact, Greek soldiers were much in demand because they had been proven against the Persian Empire as among the best in the world. In 401 B.C.E., thousands of men joined the army of Cyrus the Younger (ca. 424–401 B.C.E.), a Persian prince who was trying to grab control of the Persian Empire from his half-brother, Artaxerxes (r. 404–ca. 358 B.C.E.). One of the Greek mercenaries, Xenophon (ca. 431–ca. 352 B.C.E.), recounted in his book *Anabasis* how Greek mercenaries marched 1,500 miles to Babylon, were defeated by Artaxerxes, and marched another 2,000 miles back home.

Although the huge military operation was a failure, it featured some new developments in Greek warfare that proved successful. For example, hoplites began using lighter armor and the army began using light-armed troops (such as those with bows and arrows). These units protected the hoplite phalanxes at their flanks, or sides.

The Persian adventure also demonstrated that troops could travel with less baggage on long expeditions and find food and supplies along the way. These lessons would be put to use when Alexander the Great crossed the same territory later in the century—with far more success.

In 395 B.C.E., Sparta began the Corinthian War against Corinth and its allies, Athens, Thebes, and Argos. In 394 B.C.E., it won the largest hoplite battle since Plataea in 480 B.C.E. This victory was Sparta's last peak of power in Greece.

Sparta's army now dominated the Greek mainland. So the city-state set its sights on Greek Asia Minor, which the Persian Empire also wanted to control. Sparta was unable to take on the Persians, and

The Long Road Home

Although Xenophon was an Athenian, he spent much of his life in Sparta. When democracy was reestablished in Athens in 401, Xenophon turned his back on its new leaders and went to war in support of the Persian prince, Cyrus, in his campaign against the king of Persia, Artaxerxes II. He brought along a large force of Greek mercenaries. During the military campaign Cyrus died and the mercenaries were left leaderless. Xenophon was elected one of the generals. Fewer than 6,000 mercenaries, out of an original force of 10,000, survived. Xenophon later wrote a book about his adventure called *Anabasis*. The book was an account of the expedition, and also a tale of military virtues, discipline, leadership, and courage.

On the fifth day they did in fact reach the mountain; its name was Theches. Now as soon as the vanguard got to the top of the mountain, a great shout went up. And when Xenophon and the rearguard heard it, they imagined that other enemies were attacking in front; for enemies were following behind them from the district that was in flames. . . . But as the shout kept getting louder and nearer, as the successive ranks that came up all began to run at full speed toward the ranks ahead that were one after another joining in the shout, and as the shout kept growing far louder as the number of men grew steadily greater, it became quite clear to Xenophon that here was something of unusual importance; so he mounted a horse, took with him Lycius and the cavalry, and pushed ahead to lend aid; and in a moment they heard the soldiers shouting, "The Sea! The Sea!" and passing the word along. Then all the troops of the rearguard likewise broke into a run, and the pack animals began racing ahead and the horses. And when all had reached the summit, then indeed they fell to embracing one another, and generals and captains as well, with tears in their eyes.

(Source: Xenophon, *Anabasis*. Carleton L. Brownson, translator. Cambridge, Mass: Harvard University Press, 1998.)

withdrew in 386 B.C.E. That left the Greek city-states there to be ruled by the Persian Empire.

Although Sparta remained the dominant force on mainland Greece, wealthy Persia kept Spartan power in check by financing a new fleet of ships for Athens. A new Athenian naval league was formed. But other city-states in the league remembered Athens's aggressive leadership of Delian League, and they formed alliances designed to keep Athenian power in check. This scene was repeated many times over the first half of the fourth century B.C.E.: Sparta or Athens would gain an upper hand, until the other city-states, who may have been enemies in recent years, joined together to defeat whoever was strongest.

But Sparta, despite its military might, could never assert its leadership over fellow Greeks the way Athens had in the previous century. Sparta was unwelcoming to foreigners, and its militaristic society did not have much to offer its neighbors in the way of civics or culture. In addition, the Spartan population had been shrinking for decades. Long years of required military service meant men spent little time at home with their wives, and fewer Spartan citizens were produced with each passing decade. Sparta's army was filled with increasing numbers of non-citizens, who eventually came to greatly outnumber the Spartans themselves.

THEBAN VICTORY

In the meantime, Thebes unified the Boeotian territory for the first time. Thebes was a growing city-state whose large population benefited from the agricultural abundance of Boeotia. Its aim was defensive—because it was centrally located in mainland Greece, it was the frequent target of invasions by other Greek city-states. Boeotian hoplites were not innovative in military tactics, but they became known for their toughness in battle.

In 371 B.C.E., the Boeotians, under the leadership of Theban general Epaminondas (d. 362 B.C.E.), took on Sparta. The Thebans' goal was not so much to conquer Sparta but to prevent future Spartan invasions into Boeotia—there had been four in just the last decade.

The generally accepted military tactic, and one the Spartans also used, was to position the best companies of soldiers on a phalanx's right side. Epaminondas modified this by putting his best hoplites on the left side of his phalanx. This way, his best soldiers would fight against Sparta's best soldiers. The Boeotian phalanx was also 80 hoplites across and 50 deep, which was unusually dense.

The two armies met at Leuctra in Boeotia. The hoplites were defended by now-common cavalry and light-armed troops who shot arrows and even flung heavy stones. Although the Thebans and their Boeotian allies were outnumbered, they crashed through the Spartan phalanx, killing the Spartan king Cleombrotus (d. 371 B.C.E.) and hundreds of Sparta's best soldiers. The Spartans were shocked to find they had been defeated.

The following year, Epaminondas led his army to Laconia, where a weakened Spartan army put up only a weak defense. After the

Spartan Simplicity

Today, a *spartan* lifestyle means simplicity almost to the point where one has no pleasure. The term, of course, comes from the ancient Greek people whose citizens lived in modest homes with little difference between those who were wealthy and those who were not. In fact, there was more equality between the classes in Sparta than in a large city-state like Athens. This is because, with the Messenians serving as slaves, no Spartan had to work.

Luxury was rejected because it encouraged weakness. The Spartans also regarded cultural pursuits, such as literature, art, and music, as unnecessary. Xenophon wrote that the Spartans thought of food and drink as something of which "there should be neither too much or too little" (as quoted in *The Cambridge Illustrated History of Ancient Greece*). A typical Spartan dish was a cloudy black broth that other Greeks considered especially bad. It included port (a fortified wine), animal blood, and vinegar. *The Columbia History of the World* quotes an unnamed visitor to Sparta as saying, after sampling the local food, "Now I know why the Spartans do not fear death."

Boeotian army looted the Laconian farmlands around Sparta, Epaminondas led his troops west to Messenia. There, he freed Sparta's *helots* from three centuries of forced labor and established a strongly fortified new city for them, Messene.

Epaminondas brought his army back to the Peloponnese Peninsula several more times, eventually leaving Sparta powerless beyond Laconia. Epaminondas died in a final battle against Sparta (which was now allied with Athens against Thebes) at Mantinea in 362 B.C.E. Soon after, Theban leadership among the Greeks faded. Though brief in its term as Greece's most powerful polis, Thebes, under Epaminondas, accomplished the impressive feat not only of defeating Sparta, but also undoing the Spartans' social system, which had been based on *helot* labor.

THE MACEDONIANS

As the Greek city-states jostled for position and power, there were new threats from the north. Philip II of Macedon was adding other northern kingdoms to his own and had already gained territory in central Greece.

Macedon was a neighboring kingdom whose people spoke a Greek dialect (a different form of the same language) and considered themselves to be of Greek ancestry. Macedon's Aegean coastline had been colonized by the Greeks in previous centuries. The Macedonians were a tough people from a rugged country whose aristocracy was constantly at war among themselves. They were, however, a weak and divided state with little regional power.

In 359 B.C.E., ambitious 23-year-old Philip II, an able warrior, assumed power. Philip had a year-round professional army, and the only way to pay for it was to conquer more territory. He gained a foothold into Greece in the 350s B.C.E. The ruling aristocracy of Thessaly, the prosperous region north of Boeotia and south of Macedon, allowed Philip (whom they considered to be a fellow Greek), to take command of their alliance. Philip also used arranged marriages to build his state. By combining powerful families, he gained more control. By the end of the 340s B.C.E., Philip had consolidated his power in north and central Greece.

The most notable leader of Athens in Philip's era was the orator Demosthenes (384–322 B.C.E.). Demosthenes had been robbed of his inheritance by corrupt guardians after his father died, and he ended up writing court speeches to make a living. He overcame his initial awkwardness in public speaking by intensely practicing declamation (making formal speeches). Eventually, he earned lasting fame for his stirring addresses warning Athens about Philip's aggressive intentions.

Although the Macedonians considered themselves to be Greek, Hellenes such as Demosthenes regarded them as uncivilized. Demosthenes mobilized support for a Greek alliance to head off a Macedonian invasion into southern Greece.

When the Greeks joined forces against Philip, they faced a professional army that fought year-round. Philip took the Greek hoplite phalanx, developed in the fifth century B.C.E., and made it deadlier by using longer spears that weighed about 15 pounds. Shields were made smaller to hang from the neck or shoulders, so both hands could hold the longer spear.

Philip gave the cavalry the important role of leading off the battle by charging into enemy lines. The infantry followed, aided by archers (soldiers who shoot with bows and arrows) and other light-armed soldiers. Those soldiers could move quickly, too. They traveled light, with no servants and carrying few supplies, and they could reach any city-state on the Greek mainland within a few days.

The siege was an important military strategy of the time that was used to attack walled cities. It meant cutting off a town or fort from the outside so it could not receive supplies and the inhabitants could not escape. Siege technology traditionally used simple ladders and battering rams. Philip's military engineers designed wheeled towers that could be rolled up to walls and complex catapults (a military machine

Man of Words

Demosthenes is remembered as one of the great orators of Classical Greece, but his skills did not come naturally. He had a weak voice and tended to stutter, and had to work hard to overcome his defects. To strengthen his voice, he recited speeches and poems while running or going up steps. To lose his stutter, Demosthenes practiced by speaking with pebbles in his mouth. Today, these stories of how he improved his speech are well known. He is held up as a model for how a person can overcome personal shortcomings, and his speeches are still read as examples of powerful, effective oration.

This theater is in the city of Philippi in Macedon. It was named for Philip II, the Macedonian king who defeated an allied Greek army in 338 B.C.E. This marked the end of independent city-states in Greece.

use for throwing large objects) that hurled increasingly large objects to damage walls from up to 300 yards away. Philip was therefore able to conquer a walled city in a matter of weeks, whereas fifth-century B.C.E. Athens might spend months or even years trying to do so.

But despite all this technology, Philip's preferred method of taking a city was bribery—paying off city leaders in exchange for handing over the city. It was a style of warfare that had Demosthenes longing for the good old days, when there was plenty of "invading and ravaging" but "fighting was fair and open" (as quoted in *The Wars of the Ancient Greeks*).

Using both military tactics and bribery, Philip hoped to have a large empire with tax-paying members whose mines and harbors would be under his control. His military advances proved to be extremely effective. As Hanson points out in *The Wars of the Ancient Greeks*, 30,000 Macedonian soldiers proved "far more dangerous to Greek liberty than half a million Persians." Demosthenes' alliance was defeated by Philip's army at Chaeronea in Boeotia in 338 B.C.E.

Philip then formed a Greek-Macedonian league (which historians call the League of Corinth). He proposed that a combined army invade the Persian Empire.

With Philip II came the end of the independent Greek polis. Although a limited form of democracy continued in Athens, it and the other city-states would always be subject to other rulers. Within the next century, the cultural capital of the Greek world would be centered in a city that had not even been founded yet—Alexandria on the Mediterranean coast of Egypt.

ALEXANDER MARCHES ON PERSIA

Before he could capitalize on his victory over Greece, Philip was assassinated in 336 B.C.E. Like his father, Alexander III became king at a young age but proved that youth was no obstacle to success. Alexander ruthlessly eliminated (by murder, if necessary) all rivals for leadership over the now expanded army of Macedonians and Greeks. And he prepared to conquer the Persian Empire.

When Thebes tried to withdraw from the League of Corinth in 335 B.C.E., Alexander's army arrived at Thebes and leveled it, except for its temples and the home of the poet Pindar (ca. 520–443 B.C.E.). He spared the famous poet to demonstrate that he was, after all, a civilized Greek. Six thousand Thebans were killed, and thousands more were sold into slavery. Alexander let it be known there was no turning back from the alliance for the Greek city-states.

Alexander was cruel and ruthless, and was also a brilliant military general. Historians tend to either admire his enormous capabilities or regard him as a power-hungry tyrant. Alexander was always conscious of the image he projected, and rode into battle at the head of his cavalry (sometimes requiring rescue by his men), his cape flowing behind him and his crested helmet polished to gleam under the sun's rays. He carried a copy of the *Iliad* on all of his campaigns. Having survived close calls with death, Alexander eventually declared himself to be a son of Zeus, the king of the Greek gods.

As Alexander fought his way through Anatolia, he claimed that his aim was to free the Greek people from Persian rule. But he actually came up against—and slaughtered—thousands of Greek merce-

Alexander the Great is shown on one of the millions of coins that featured his face. Alexander's conquests spread Greek culture throughout much of the world.

nary soldiers. Beginning at the Granicus River in 334 B.C.E., Alexander's Macedonian-Greek army smashed all Persian opposition in Asia Minor before making his way to cities such as Tyre (in modern-day Lebanon).

By 331 B.C.E., he had conquered Egypt and founded one of the many cities named Alexandria that would dot the map of the world after his death. (Alexandria, Egypt remains an important city today, with a population of more than 3 million. It is the second-largest city in Egypt and its main seaport.) When Alexander inflicted a huge defeat on the Persian army of Darius III (380–330 B.C.E.) at Gaugamela (in modern-day northern Iraq, near Mosul) in 331 B.C.E., he declared himself king of the Persian Empire. He needed thousands of mules and camels to haul away the huge Persian treasury of gold and other valuables.

THE HELLENISTIC AGE

Although Alexander left much destruction in his wake, he and his successors also founded cities that spread the best features of Greek civilization and served as new markets and ports for Greece. He had envisioned a vast empire, but Alexander did not plan for anyone to rule after him. Alexander's wife, Roxane, gave birth to his son a few months after he died (the boy was murdered in 310 B.C.E.), but the lands he conquered were divided up among his top commanders.

Alexander's generals formed three new kingdoms that roughly encompassed the areas of his conquests. Antigonus II (320–239 B.C.E.), grandson of Alexander's general Antigonus (ca. 382–301 B.C.E.), became king and heir to the throne of Macedon and maintained control over Greece. Seleucus (ca. 358–281 B.C.E.) took over what had been the Persian Empire. Ptolemy (ca. 367–282) became king of Egypt. Their descendants would inherit these kingdoms until the Roman Empire ruled the Mediterranean world.

The city-states of Greece were no longer independent. Like their neighbors in other ancient civilizations, they were now part of one large kingdom. And because of Alexander, their culture became the foundation of what is today called the Hellenistic Age. (The term was used by 19th-century historians to describe the 293 years between Alexander's death and 30 B.C.E., when the last of the Hellenistic kingdoms fell to the Roman Empire.)

Much of the wealth grabbed from the Persian Empire by Alexander was now divided up among the three kingdoms, boosting their economies and providing employment through extensive public building projects. By the third century B.C.E., the Greek language had become the common language of international relations from Egypt and Jerusalem up to the Black Sea in the north and to the border of modern-day India in the east. Since everyone spoke the same language, it was much easier to exchange ideas throughout the Hellenistic world. Greek immigrants moved to the cities in these Hellenistic kingdoms, exchanging cultural and social ideas with the local peoples.

Although many Greek city-states were now ruled by Macedonian kings, parts of Greece remained free. In the regions of Aetolia and Achaea, city-states joined together in leagues with a strong central government. The member city-states also kept their own governments. The federal organization of the Achaean League, described by the Greek historian Polybios (ca. 200–118 B.C.E.), provided inspiration to the Founding Fathers of the United States.

AN INVITATION TO ROME

The Romans became increasingly powerful in the Hellenistic world. By the middle of the third century B.C.E., they controlled most of Italy. When Philip V (r. 221–179 B.C.E.) of Macedon tried to expand his territory into Ionia around 200 B.C.E., leaders in Pergamum, Athens, and Rhodes asked Rome to help them turn him back. Rome provided successful help, and granted the cities it aided their independence. But it was now obvious that a new power had emerged in the Mediterranean.

By the middle of the second century B.C.E., Rome had conquered Macedon and most of Greece. When Corinth attempted to rebel in 146 B.C.E., it was destroyed by Rome.

Rome's power would last longer than that of Athens or the other Greek city-states, for a variety of reasons. Rome had united the other cities of Italy—something the Greek city-states had never been able to accomplish in Greece. Rome was also generous in granting rights to foreigners. From this broad base of manpower, they could form an army large enough to conquer the Hellenistic world. And Hellenistic warfare had grown clumsy, while the Romans improved it by simplifying tactics.

Hellenistic soldiers now fought with even longer spears, up to 20 feet long, and the once-effective tactic of using cavalry to burst through enemy lines was not much used. Roman soldiers also carried smaller spears that they threw at their enemy. Then they moved in for close combat using the *gladius,* a double-edged steel sword (from which we get the word *gladiator*) that was much easier to handle than the long Greek spear, and which inflicted much damage. In 30 B.C.E., the last of the Hellenistic kingdoms—Egypt under Queen Cleopatra—was defeated by the Roman Empire.

PART · II

SOCIETY AND CULTURE

POLITICS AND SOCIETY IN ANCIENT GREECE

EVERYDAY LIFE IN ANCIENT GREECE

GREEK ART, PHILOSOPHY, AND SCIENCE

CHAPTER 4

POLITICS AND SOCIETY IN ANCIENT GREECE

ATHENS OF THE FIFTH CENTURY B.C.E. REPRESENTS WHAT we today consider to be best about the politics of ancient Greece. The democratic government that developed there inspired later political thinkers in Europe, North America, and other regions who were seeking to build free and fair societies.

Yet during Athens's early history, the city resisted the gradual economic and political compromises that enabled the rich and poor to live together peacefully in other Greek city-states. The rich in Athens tried to hold on to power for too long, and the result was a radical democratic revolution in the sixth century B.C.E.

It is important to remember that not all ancient Greeks practiced democracy the way the Athenians did. Many Greek city-states never developed a democracy at all. There were always many Greeks, including some in Athens, who considered democracy to be rule by the mob—dangerous, unstable, and unwise.

KINGS AND NOBLES

Like other ancient civilizations of the Near East, the early Greek communities were first ruled by chieftains or kings. The kings led groups of families to new settlements and helped organize them militarily so they could defend themselves from outsiders. According to Aristotle in his *Politics* (as cited by John V. A. Fine in *The Ancient Greeks*), a king ruled with the consent of the people and had limited powers, "with the king acting as general and judge and the head of religious obser-

OPPOSITE
The ancient Greeks were practical people and business came first. The scene on this sixth-century B.C.E. Greek cup shows Arcesilas II (ca. 560–550 B.C.E.), the king of Cyrene, watching cargo being weighed and loaded onto his ship. The cargo is a medicinal plant called silphium. Silphium exports were critical to the economy of Cyrene.

The Ethnos

City-states did not develop everywhere in ancient Greece. Parts of the Peloponnesus Peninsula and northern Greece were dotted with small villages that lacked a central town that could serve as a political and economic capital. The Greeks called these regions the *ethne* (the plural of *ethnos*), which means "tribes" or "peoples." The residents within one *ethnos* shared a cultural background, but separate villages rarely took united action. Living in an *ethnos* was considered a mark of backwardness, since the people in *ethne* did not develop complex political systems.

The word *ethnos* led to the English word *ethnic* and the prefix *ethno,* which refers to a race of people or a cultural group. *Ethnocentric,* for example, describes someone who believes his or her ethnic group is better than all others. *Ethnography* is the study of human cultures.

vances." In his role as judge, the king settled arguments between *oikoi,* or households.

These early Greek kingdoms were not large. They usually consisted of scattered *oikoi* that relied on farming to survive. But as the disorder of the Dark Age ended, the population of the kingdoms grew, and the first towns grew up around the king's residence.

The kings relied on the advice of the heads of the wealthiest *oikoi* to run the government. With their wealth and political influence, these advisors formed an elite class known as the *basilees,* with the king called a *basileus.* The *basilees* formed the nobility. The leaders of this nobility called themselves *aristoi,* "the best," leading to the English word *aristocrat.* The Greek aristocrats looked down on what they called *hoi polloi,* "the many." That term is still used today to describe large masses of poor or powerless people.

THE RISE OF THE *POLIS*

The town where a king and his advisors lived became the heart of the political unit called the polis, or city. Over time, farms surrounding the city center joined the polis, creating a city-state, which the Greek still called polis.

The rural *oikoi* who joined a polis wanted the security that came with being part of a larger community. At the same time, these farmers were used to living without direct rule, and they wanted some say in how their government was run. Assemblies, where male citizens gathered to debate public issues, were already a key part of Greek politics in the eighth century B.C.E.

As the *poleis* (plural of polis) developed, the *basilees* in most city-states asserted their growing political and economic strength and forced the *basileus* from power. The details of this transition are not clear. But by the seventh century B.C.E., the aristocrats as a group controlled the *poleis,* with several officials sharing the duties once held by the *basileus.*

The number of government officials, or magistrates, grew as a city-state grew. Athens, for example, had many more magistrates, with specific duties, than did smaller city-states. After leaving public office, the most important magistrates sat on a council that passed laws and directed most government affairs. Council members often served for life. With the rise of the aristocracy and the councils, the assemblies—and thus the common farmers—lost some political influence for a time.

The polis was both a religious and a political entity, and individual city-states had a particular patron god. Athena was the patron of both Sparta and Athens. Several cities in Asia Minor had as their patron Zeus's brother Poseidon, who ruled the seas. A polis, the Greeks believed, would not prosper, nor would its citizens, without paying proper honor to the various gods in charge of the universe. So a series of festivals with various rituals to please and honor the gods was built into the social life of the polis.

Aristotle believed the polis reflected a natural law: Humans are political creatures and are only complete when they live together in a community. In his *Politics* he wrote, "He who is unable to live in society, or who has no need because he is sufficient for himself, must be either a beast or a god: he is no part of a state. A social instinct is implanted in all men. . . ." (as quoted in *Ancient Thought: Plato and Aristotle*).

Yet each Greek polis cherished its independence from its neighbors, and some developed along very different political lines. Sparta, for example, was kept very strict, with two kings who shared power, while Athens created the environment that brought about democracy, drama, comedy, and philosophy.

Despite the achievements of Athens, however, some historians have argued that the polis was always destined to fail. The very independence that encouraged experimentation and diversity of thought also discouraged the tendency to work together as a united nation.

CITIZENS AND SOLDIERS

Within the *poleis* were both citizens and non-citizens. The non-citizens were either foreigners or slaves. Unlike most of the world throughout most of history before and after Greece, a person did not have to own land to become a citizen. However, a citizen's rights and privileges, varied based on social status and gender.

Female citizens could not take part in politics, and only the wealthiest male citizens could hold political office. Middle-class Greeks could vote in the assemblies, but the poorest citizens could not. In their book *Ancient Greece: A Political, Social, and Cultural History*, Sarah B. Pomeroy, Stanley M. Burstein, Walter Donlan, and Jennifer Tolbert Roberts write that the history of Greece from 700 to 500 B.C.E. "is the

IN THEIR OWN WORDS

Men of Strength

Alcaeus (sixth century B.C.E.) was a poet-soldier from the city of Mytilene on the island of Lesbos, one of the Greek islands on the coast of Ionia (present-day Turkey). Many of his poems reveal a life of fighting, drinking, and enjoying the company of women. His poetry also describes hoplite warfare and the rise of tyrants that were typical in early sixth century B.C.E. Greece. In one poem, he wrote of the importance of "men of strength" within a city.

> Not home with beautiful roofs,
> nor walls of permanent stone,
> nor canals and piers for ships
> make the city—but men of strength.
>
> Not stone and timber, nor skill
> of carpenter—but men brave,
> who will handle sword and spear.
> With these you have city and walls.

(Source: Atchity, Kenneth J., editor, *The Classical Greek Reader*. New York: Henry Holt and Company, 1996.)

struggle of the middle and lower classes to gain an equal share in the governance of their *poleis*." Their success was mixed, since some oligarchy states remained after this era. Only a few *poleis*, such as Athens, developed true democracy.

For some Greek citizens, the military was their path to greater political influence. Aristocrats were only as powerful as the polis they controlled, and the rulers needed strong fighting forces to defend their city or expand its influence. Most city-states relied on their citizens to serve as soldiers, as opposed to hiring and training professional troops.

Around 700 B.C.E., Greek warfare began to feature the hoplites. These citizen-soldiers began to demand a greater say in political affairs, since they were risking their lives to defend both their own and the aristocrats' lands. The oligarchy had to give in, since they needed the military support of the middle class.

The hoplite armies led to shifts in social attitudes. Discipline was a key part of the hoplites' battlefield success. For the first time, aristocrats had to learn to work well with members of the lower classes. Middle-class soldiers showed that they could match the bravery and skill of their supposed "superiors."

This battlefield experience fueled the call for greater political equality, and shaped the concept that courage in war, not noble birth, determined a man's worth to his polis. Soldiers fought for the honor of the polis, although they might win personal honor for individual heroism. Many Greeks known today for their writings and philosophy—

Socrates, Sophocles, Thucydides, and Demosthenes, for example—were also soldiers.

CHANGES IN ATHENS

Modern historians know more about the political and social life of Athens than those of any other Greek polis. Its history offers the best example of how the average citizens gained political power, leading to a democratic state. The process of empowering citizens was speeded up by Solon, a poet-politician who was given the task of trying to settle down the angry lower classes of Athens.

Solon was appointed as sole *archon*, or ruling aristocrat, in 594 B.C.E. He truly sought to defend the poor from the abuses of the rich, which included forcing people who owed money into slavery. In one poem, Solon complained, "The citizens themselves, through their foolish acts, are willing to destroy the great city, yielding to their desire for wealth" (as quoted in *The Classical Greek Reader*).

Solon ended the practice of enslaving debtors and canceled debts that the poor still owed. At the same time, the aristocrats would not give up too much of their overall influence. For the most part, Solon's changes were moderate, not radical. He wanted to preserve the existing society by improving it, not create something totally new.

Solon created a set of written laws that spelled out the rights and duties of Greek citizens. He divided the citizens into four distinct classes, based on wealth. At the top were aristocrats known as the *pentakosiomedimnoi*—a Greek word that means their farms produced at least 500 bushels of crops a year. These aristocrats paid higher taxes than other citizens did, but they also held the most important public offices and elected the *archons*.

Beneath them were the *hippeis*, or "horsemen," whose farms produced between 300 and 499 bushels of produce a year. This upper-middle class provided most of the cavalry for the Athenian army, as well as many hoplites. They also could be important magistrates and serve as *archons*.

The next class was the *zeugitai*, which translates as "oxmen." Members of this class could afford to keep teams of oxen but not horses, and their farms produced between 200 and 299 bushels of crops a year. The *zeugitai* were usually hoplites. In government, they could be less-important magistrates.

At the bottom were farmers and laborers called *thetes*, or "poor freemen." In the military, they served as lightly armored foot soldiers or oarsmen on *triremes*.

The *thetes*, along with members of the other three classes, could participate in the Athenian Assembly. The Assembly, called the Ekklesia in Greek, continued to function as a forum for public debate, as it had for centuries across the Greek city-states. The Assembly also took on a new role under Solon: His legal system allowed all male citizens, rich and poor, to appeal decisions made by the *archons* and challenge the corrupt acts of magistrates. These appeals and challenges were heard in the Assembly. And that meant all male citizens from every class were potential jurors.

Every male citizen, not just victims of crime or their relatives, also had the right to bring someone to court for committing a crime. Before this, families took action against each other when the member of one family wronged the member of another family. As Sarah Pomeroy and her co-authors write in *The Ancient Greeks*, "justice was now the business of the community . . . as a whole," not just individuals or their families.

The Athenian government during Solon's time also included a council called the Aeropagus. Its members were all former *archons* and they influenced which laws were passed. Members served for life, and traditionally they came from the oldest and most powerful families in Athens. Since Solon expanded the pool of potential *archons*, drawing from the upper-middle class as well as the aristocracy, some of the old families lost political influence in the Aeropagus. Still, it normally favored the interests of the wealthy. The evidence is not clear, but under Solon the Assembly seems to have had some role in electing certain officials and shaping laws.

Solon's reforms also affected the economy and citizenship. He promoted the export of a key Athenian product, olive oil, while limiting the foreign sale of barley. Historians believe that grain may have been in short supply at the time, and the polis needed all the barley it could grow to feed its own citizens. Solon also wanted skilled foreigners to come to Athens, so he tempted them with citizenship if they and their families became permanent residents of Attica. This policy angered some Athenians, who considered citizenship a privileged status. Later rulers ended the practice.

CLASSICAL DEMOCRACY

Cleisthenes, who was in power by 510 B.C.E., continued the progression toward true democracy in Athens. He wanted to break up the old village system of *demes*, which was based on family ties within certain geographic regions. His new system split Attica into three regions, called the city, the shore, and the inland. Within each region were 10 areas called *trittys* (Greek for "thirds").

Cleisthenes then created 10 new tribes by combining one *trittys* from each region to form a tribe. Citizens were now allied by their political participation in one of the new tribes, rather than by family ties. The old aristocrats could no longer count on family influence and regional power to control political events.

Cleisthenes also created a new council, called the *boule* in Greek and commonly known today as the Council of 500. Each year, each tribe selected 50 male citizens to sit on the Council of 500. They were chosen at random. The new council proposed issues for the Assembly to debate, met foreign diplomats, and oversaw the appointment of tax collectors.

In general, Cleisthenes's reforms expanded government involvement for Athenians. The members of the *boule* changed often, since they were selected at random, and each of the 10 tribes also elected different officials for the military. All of the reforms were approved by the Assembly, reflect-

This tablet, called an *ostrakhon*, shows that a man named Themistokles was "ostracized" in 472 B.C.E. Who was ostracized was determined by a vote. The ostracized person was sent away from the polis for 10 years.

Ostracism

Among the new elements the *archon* Cleisthenes seems to have introduced to Athenian government was ostracism. Under this system, each year the citizens of Athens could vote to send one person out of the *polis* for 10 years. After the 10 years passed, the ostracized person could return to Athens and reclaim whatever property he had owned before leaving.

This system let the Athenians banish a person they perceived to be a threat to social order. Ten years, the Greeks assumed, was long enough for a potential tyrant to lose influence in the community. Today, ostracism usually occurs within a particular social group, as its members choose to exclude or ignore someone who has upset other group members.

ing a wide level of support among the population as a whole. Herodotus, in Book Five of *The Histories,* notes that Cleisthenes was deliberately trying to win popular support to gain the upper hand over his aristocratic rivals. The plan worked, because "once he had won the ordinary people over, he was far more powerful than his political opponents."

Cleisthenes' changes also set Athens on a stronger path to democracy. Government by the *demos* still faced threats, though, because some aristocrats considered uneducated citizens to be incapable of correctly using the decision-making power they were given.

In the first half of the fifth century B.C.E., the Athenian general and politician Ephialtes (d. ca. 460 B.C.E.), weakened the Aeropagus. The details of his reforms are unclear, but he seems to have convinced the Assembly to give some of the Aeropagus's powers to the *boule,* the courts, and the Assembly itself. Anti-democratic aristocrats then had Ephialtes assassinated—an extreme reaction to his democratic reforms. Despite this, the trend toward giving more decision-making power to the citizens of the polis continued. Partly, this was because the labor of the *demos*—the common men—was needed to drive the scores of *triremes* that now patrolled the Aegean Sea and the other coasts of Greece.

PERICLEAN DEMOCRACY

During the time of Ephialtes's reform, Pericles was a major supporter of democracy. He became the most influential Athenian leader during the Classical period of Greek history. In his *History of the Peloponnesian War,* Thucydides called Pericles "the leading man of his time among the Athenians and the most powerful both in action and in debate." He was one of 10 *strategoi,* the men elected to direct military affairs in Athens. Pericles used his intelligence and personality to dominate Athenian politics from about 460 to 429 B.C.E.

In the government that developed under Pericles, all male citizens could participate in the Assembly after serving two years in the military. The Assembly met four times each month. Out of a possible 40,000 male citizens, 6,000 were needed to lawfully carry out a few of the Assembly's duties, such as granting citizenship to a foreigner. Other common activities could be carried out with even fewer people present. A council of educated and upper-class *archons* with the wealth and leisure time to serve in unpaid government positions still oversaw much of the government, but the Assembly's vote always ruled.

One important reform begun under Pericles was paying citizens to serve on juries. Later, people were also paid for attending the Assembly and holding some civic positions, and could eat at public expense while serving in the *boule*. These payments further opened up participation in the government, since a working man could now afford to give up a full-time job and play an active role in public affairs. When government jobs were unpaid, only the wealthy could afford to spend more than a day or two working in the government.

THE COURTS

The court system under Pericles also changed, although the first reforms were probably carried out by Ephialtes. These changes increased the role of the *demos* in judicial matters. All male citizens were eligible for jury duty, and a pool of 6,000 jurors was always available.

Each of the 10 tribes chose 600 jurors each year, picking from a group of citizens who volunteered to serve. The chosen jurors were divided into smaller groups of perhaps several hundred per trial. With hundreds of jurors, it was very difficult and expensive to use bribery to influence the outcome of a trial.

Like the Assembly, the jury system called on a wide variety of Athenian citizens, rich and poor. Under Pericles, jurors began receiving wages for the day they served on a trial. Trials took place in one day and each side got an opportunity to speak. Punishments for the guilty consisted of death, banishment (sending someone away from the country), or a fine.

In a trial, as in the Assembly, the art of persuasive speaking was of great value. Sometimes a person standing trial might have a speech written for him or even read for him by someone skilled in rhetoric—the art of speaking or writing effectively.

GREEK SOCIETY

In general, there were three types of Greek city-state residents. The first type included citizen men, women, and children. The next type were *metics*, who could be citizens of a different city-state or from a foreign country. The third type were slaves, who could be fellow Greeks, but were more likely war captives (men, women, and children) from another country.

President of the Assembly

The Assembly's president for the day was chosen at random from among those present. That meant any one of Athens's citizens, many of whom could not read, had a chance to preside over the Assembly for a day. This benefit of Athenian citizenship (for males over age 20, at least) was unique in the ancient world, and throughout the world for centuries to come.

While female citizens had few rights, male citizens were allowed—even expected—to attend Assembly meetings and vote on important issues. (This would be similar to American citizens being allowed to show up in the U.S. Capitol building in Washington and vote on new laws in Congress.) For example, a vote of the Assembly decided whether or not the Athenian navy would embark on a risky venture during the Peloponnesian War in 415 B.C.E.

In *Daily Life in Greece at the Time of Pericles*, Robert Flaceliere estimates that in Athens in the mid-fifth century B.C.E., there were 40,000 male citizens and 20,000 male *metics*, and about 140,000 women and children citizens and *metics*. There may have been 300,000 slaves throughout the city-state, for a total of half a million people. Of these fewer than 10 percent had the right to vote.

Citizens enjoyed the most rights and freedoms—even the poorest laborers. When *metics* moved to a city-state where they would be considered a foreigner, they gave up any rights to own property or participate in the democratic process. But in general, *metics* were still valued residents and often brought a variety of vital professional and manual skills with them.

Slaves had few if any rights. The more fortunate ones had some degree of freedom of movement, or lived with a family that treated them decently.

At the top of the citizen pyramid were the aristocrats, whose families had provided government and military leadership for many generations. They lived off income from land the family had held for many generations. Their land was worked by slaves, as well as perhaps by citizens or *metic* laborers.

The upper classes of Athens made contributions to their city-state that improved the quality of life for all residents. They might fund the building and manning of a *trireme*, or pay for a religious festival or the creation of a public park, or have a covered walkway in the agora (marketplace) built, which offered shelter from the rain and sun. The wealthiest classes also paid for such day-to-day things as garbage removal and maintaining water supplies.

Athens's wealthiest citizens lived in comfortable but modest homes. Athenians did not feel it was appropriate for people to live in mansions or palaces. That luxury was reserved for the gods. Their most outstanding architectural and artistic efforts therefore went into their religious buildings, which were considered homes for their gods. In fact, any aristocrat who was interested in serving in the government, and was therefore dependent on the ordinary citizens for support, knew not to show off his wealth. If a citizen wanted the respect of the *demos*, he spent his personal wealth on public projects.

Athens's well-educated aristocrats made enough income from their land to live a life of leisure. They could devote time to leading the Athenian government or military without pay. In fact, the true sign of a gentleman was leisure time. Any sort of work, even something as admired as producing fine artwork or architecture, or a profession that required much study, such as that of a physician, was looked down upon by the upper class. A true gentleman never used his hands, however much intellect or skill it required, unless it was for military service or athletics.

Most men, however, had to work for a living. A hierarchy existed among those who worked in ancient Greece. Farmers who owned a plot of land looked down upon craftsmen, and both of them looked down upon traders and importers, who did not actually produce anything. Working for another person instead of oneself was considered a humiliation, so all of the above looked down upon the man who had to hire himself out to someone else for a living. On the other hand, all of these groups of people could participate in their city-state's government and legal system, which is more than the *metic*, slave, or woman citizen could do.

Historians think it is possible that the prosperity of ancient Greece, beginning in the Archaic Period, must have meant low unemployment rates. This would have been especially true for workers in carpentry and other building trades, and smithing, or metalworking. Many of the *metics* who flocked to Athens were unable to purchase their own homes, so some citizens became newly wealthy by renting homes to the foreigners. Renting out slaves provided another possibility for a good income for citizens and *metics*. Newly wealthy citizens often then became manufacturers or traders, while the old aristocrats would never engage in commerce because of its low social status.

METICS

By the middle of the fifth century B.C.E., there were about half as many male *metics* in Athens as there were male citizens. Early in the sixth century B.C.E., Solon's liberal citizenship laws had encouraged their immigration to Athens. But 150 years later, citizenship was considered more valuable and Pericles restricted citizenship to the children of two Athenian parents. Yet *metics* still flocked to Athens, drawn by the economic opportunities they found there.

Metics had no real political power or rights, but many grew rich as manufacturers or in commerce or banking. Socrates had a friend, Cephalus from Syracuse, whose shield factory employed more than 100 slaves. Wealthy *metics*, in fact, had the same kinds of public obligations as wealthy citizens, and helped fund civic projects.

In the years 401 and 400 B.C.E. the Athenian government awarded several *metics* citizenship for their help in overthrowing the Thirty Tyrants—the oppressive rulers installed by Sparta. The occupations listed for them included cook, carpenter, gardener, baker, household servant, and nut-seller.

Some of Athens's more notable *metics* included the doctor Hippocrates (ca. 460–ca. 377 B.C.E.), the historian Herodotus, and Aristotle, the great fourth-century B.C.E. philosopher.

SLAVERY IN GREECE

Slavery played a vital economic role in ancient Greece. Slaves generally were foreign war captives or the wives and children of the Greeks' slain enemies. But sometimes Greeks, such as the Spartans and the Messenians, enslaved fellow Greeks following a raid or battle.

Much like Greek citizens, the life of a slave could vary from decent to miserable. A decent life could be had if a slave worked in a home in town or in the country, where one might become almost a family member. Sometimes older male slaves accompanied their master's sons to school and had the authority to discipline the boys if necessary. And those who worked for the government or a large manufacturer who owned many slaves enjoyed as independent a life as a slave could have.

Greek slaves had no legal rights and they sometimes endured abusive owners who beat them or forced them to have sex. Slaves were owned by the polis or by individuals. Those belonging to the polis had more status and more freedom, often living independently. They might be put to work, for example, working as policemen in Athens or cleaning up garbage, or they might be assigned to maintain the temple of the polis's deity.

Female slaves were often found in households or working for a merchant in the agora. Educated slaves were valuable as tutors for children in upper-class homes. Slaves often worked alongside their owners on small farms in the countryside or at crafts such as pottery, sculpting, and metalworking. They might be as skilled as their owners at these crafts. While construction of a temple called the Erechtheum was under way in the late fifth century B.C.E. Athens, detailed construction records show that much of the intricate woodworking and stone carv-

Shown on this krater are a master (right) and a slave (left). Most slaves were war captives from foreign countries.

ing that decorated the building was done by slaves. Hoplite soldiers would have had little strength left for fighting if not for the slaves who carried much of their equipment from place to place.

Occasionally, slaves managed to improve their status. A few were able to earn money and save enough to buy their freedom. Some older slaves were freed by their masters as a reward for good service. The freed slaves were considered *metics*, which meant they could not vote and they needed special permission to own land. One rare case of a slave earning citizenship in Athens involved a man named Pasion (fourth century B.C.E.), who was freed and then managed the bank of his former owners.

The most miserable slaves in ancient Greece worked in the mines. Long days in the harsh conditions of the mine made for a short life. But in general Athens did not have the problem of slave rebellions that Sparta did with its helots. While helots were not technically slaves, they were still brutalized by the Spartans. The Athenians had fewer slaves than the Spartans did helots, and they did not treat their slaves as harshly as the Spartans did their helots.

Without *helots*, Sparta might never have achieved its military strength. And without slaves, Athens may not have had enough silver to outfit its navy, which played such a key role in the city-state's rise to an empire.

Ancient civilizations, including that of the Greeks, seldom questioned the ethics of slavery. It was an accepted part of life. In fact, Aristotle argued in *Politics* that some people are naturally inferior and are fit only for slavery. He said the fact that Greek slaves were usually foreigners made them uncivilized, therefore inferior, therefore deserving of slavery.

THE BUSINESS OF ANCIENT GREECE

In addition to their other cultural contributions, the Greeks also "laid foundations of modern commerce," according to historians Marjorie Quennell and C. H. B. Quennell in their book *Everyday Things in Ancient Greece.* For wealthy Greeks, land ownership remained the main source of wealth. The distribution of land varied from region to region. Athens, for example, had a much larger number of landowners, and each owned a relatively smaller piece of land. In the lush farm country of Boeotia, most of the land remained in the possession of a small number of aristocratic families.

Farming, not trade, was the foundation of the ancient Greek economy. Yet the Greeks were unable to grow all their own food. They developed an import-export trade that was supported by their skill at sea travel and by new Greek ports established by colonists around the Mediterranean.

Scenes of trade were popular as decorations on Greek pottery. For example, a sixth-century B.C.E. drinking cup found in Sparta was illustrated with a detailed trading scene from the Greek settlement at Cyrene on the North African coast. In the scene, a ship is being loaded with a shipment of silphion, a plant that is now extinct. It was similar to fennel and was prized as a medicine. The local king is watching as the cargo is weighed, then taken below deck to the ship's hold.

Greek wine, olive oil, and prized pottery were exchanged for wheat from southern Russia, fish, timber, and exotic products from the East such as spices, perfumes, and medicines. The mines of Greece, such as the silver mine in Attica and a rich source of copper at Cyprus, provided another resource for trade. And throughout the ancient world, slaves were always a profitable "product." The Athenian agora held a large slave market each month at the time of the full moon.

GREEK MONEY

By 600 B.C.E., trade was flourishing in and out of Greek ports. This was true both on the mainland and abroad in the Greek colonies. About this time, the Greeks began using coins. (Previously, all trade was conducted using the barter system, where goods were exchanged for other goods of equal value.)

Herodotus credits the wealthy Lydian kingdom in Anatolia, west of Ionia, with introducing coins as currency in the sixth century B.C.E. The Lydian coins were made of electrum, a combination of gold and silver, and they were stamped with an official seal to prove they were genuine. Even so, until the Persian Wars there was little money actually circulating in Greece.

When silver was discovered at Laurium, Athenian silver coins became common. They were stamped with an owl on one side (a symbol of Athena) and the head of the goddess Athena on the other. The government symbols and heads of famous people found on today's coins trace their roots to that practice.

This Greek coin shows an owl, one of the symbols of the goddess Athena. The Greeks began using currency around 600 B.C.E. The practice of stamping coins with government symbols began in Athens.

One silver drachma was about what one skilled worker earned each day. Six thousand drachmas equaled one talent. An obol was one-sixth of a drachma, and bought enough bread for one day. One was equal to several copper coins. Each polis had its own coinage, and with all the money that began circulating in Greece, exchanging money and banking became common professions later in the fifth century B.C.E. It often was the work of *metics* or even educated slaves.

During the Peloponnesian War, Sparta helped Athenian slaves escape the silver mines, and for a time silver coins were replaced by bronze ones. The playwright Aristophanes (ca. 450–ca. 388 B.C.E.) has a humorous scene in one of his plays in which a character is just about to pay for some bread with his copper coins when someone announces that silver is now Athens's official currency. If only he had bought the bread a few moments sooner!

SPARTA, A SEPARATE WORLD

By the time the Roman Empire gained control of Greece in the second century B.C.E., Sparta was no longer a military powerhouse. Instead it had become a kind of tourist attraction. This was due not only to its once-legendary military might among the Greek city-states, but also its unique society.

Greek tradition claimed the Spartans descended from the Dorians, the invaders who supposedly swooped down from the north at the beginning of the Dark Age. Sparta began as a few villages that grew into a city-state and eventually conquered the southern Peloponnesian area of Laconia.

The Spartan social system developed gradually from about 650 to 450 B.C.E. The reforms that changed Sparta into a military state are traditionally associated with Spartan King Lycurgus, who is said to have lived around 650 B.C.E. The Spartans believed the god Apollo approved Lycurgus's reforms through the oracle at Delphi.

It is not clear if Lycurgus (his name means "he who brings into being the works of a wolf") was an actual person.

IN THEIR OWN WORDS

The Spartan Look

In his book *On the Polity of the Spartans*, historian Xenophon discusses the Spartan's political and social system. He traces its roots back to Lycurgus, the legendary king and lawgiver of Sparta. In this section, he describes some typical aspects of a Spartan soldier's appearance.

For the actual encounter under arms, the following inventions are attributed to Lycurgus: the soldier has a crimson-colored uniform and a heavy shield of bronze; his theory being that such equipment has no sort of feminine association, and is altogether most warrior-like. It is most quickly burnished [polished]; it is least readily soiled. He further permitted those who were about the age of early manhood to wear their hair long. For so, he conceived, they would appear of larger stature, more free and indomitable, and of a more terrible aspect. . . . Further, the law enjoins upon all Spartans, during the whole period of the campaign, the constant practice of gymnastic exercises, whereby their pride in themselves is increased, and they appear freer and of a more liberal aspect than the rest of the world.

(Source: Xenophon, *On the Polity of the Spartans*. "The Spartan War Machine," Ancient History Sourcebook. Available online. URL: http://www.fordham.edu/halsall/ancient/xenophon-spartanwar.html. Accessed April 16, 2008.)

However, the Spartans certainly believed he was, and he is mentioned by the ancient historians Herodotus, Xenophon, and Plutarch. They believed it was Lycurgus who laid the foundations of daily life for the militaristic Spartans, setting up rules for everything from the education of young boys to eating meals together.

Sparta was the only Greek polis that kept a monarchy. It set up a system with two kings, perhaps as an early compromise between some of the larger villages. These two rulers had equal power. One focused on wars and foreign affairs while the other dealt with domestic issues. They also served as the religious leaders of the polis.

The Spartan governing body consisted of the kings and a council of 28 male citizens. Collectively, the kings and the council members were called the Council of Elders. Any male over age 60 could enter the elections for the council, but most members came from the aristocracy. Sparta also had an assembly of all male citizens over the age of 30, which voted on the laws proposed by the Council of Elders. The council, however, had supreme power, because it could reject decisions made by the assembly.

The Spartan government also had five *ephors*, which means "overseers." They supervised the kings and the council by keeping track of laws and making sure they were followed. Each year the male citizens elected new *ephors*. The *ephors* provided some check on the power of the aristocracy. Sparta's laws were not written down, but were learned by children in song form and passed down orally over the generations.

No Place for Debate

Unlike Athenian citizens, Spartans were not allowed to debate in their assembly. They simply voted yes or no on the laws presented to them. Spartans were expected to obey the law and not question their rulers' actions. They were said to dislike debate and rhetoric.

The Spartan tendency to use simple language or seldom speak led to the English word *laconic*, which means using as few words as possible, sometimes to the point of being rude. The word *laconic* traces its roots to *Laconia*, the region of Greece that Sparta dominated.

CHAPTER 5

EVERYDAY LIFE IN ANCIENT GREECE

EVERYDAY LIFE VARIED GREATLY AMONG THE ANCIENT Greeks, depending on which economic group one was born into or whether one lived in the city or the country. Within an Athenian aristocratic family, for example, a woman citizen lived more comfortably, materially, than a poorer citizen who sold items at the market.

Country folk in Attica dreaded leaving their peaceful farms during the Peloponnesian War to seek safety within Athens's city walls. But city dwellers enjoyed the stimulating environment of the bustling agora. Urban life also offered greater opportunity to see various competitions during the frequent religious festivals that occurred on a much grander scale in the city than in the country *demes* (villages).

EVERYDAY LIFE IN ATHENS

Fifth and fourth century B.C.E. Athens was dirty and crowded, and dangerous after dark. As the city began spreading out from the Acropolis (the hill at the center of Athens) at the end of the Dark Age, the growth was not planned or organized. So after about three centuries, the glorious sights atop the Acropolis looked down upon a densely packed patchwork of little houses along narrow, winding, crowded streets.

Poorer people lived in homes made of mud brick or stone that were so rickety thieves could enter them by breaking through a wall. Some of the poorest homes were put up against the side of a rock or in small cave-like openings of a rock wall, from which two or three small rooms were fashioned. If rent was overdue, the landlord could remove the door or the roof, or block the tenant's access to water.

OPPOSITE

A tuna merchant chops the head off a fish in this vase painting from ancient Greece. Painted pottery was an important export. It is also an important resource for historians today, because it shows many scenes from Greek life.

Some Athenian dwellings were similar to modern apartment buildings, with several families or tenants having their own rooms in the same large building. Xenophon estimated that in his day, there were about 10,000 dwellings in Athens, most of them humble.

The agora, or marketplace, was the heart of the city. Commerce of every kind was conducted there and men met to discuss politics and culture. It was considered impolite for women to be seen there, though poorer women and working women had little choice. Younger men were discouraged from visiting the agora until later in the day. Ideally, house slaves or married men did the household shopping and errands there.

Outside the city walls was the main cemetery. A little farther west was the *deme* of Colonus and just past that was the Academy, a park-like area dedicated to Athena with a grove of 12 sacred olive trees. It was from those trees that athletic winners at the Panathenaic games received prizes of olive oil. The Academy (where the philosopher Plato founded his school in 387 B.C.E.) was a popular place for strolls. It was also the site of a gymnasium that included a running track and a wrestling arena.

Going much farther out into the country was difficult, because roads were rough and could only be traveled on foot or by donkey. In the dark, roads outside the city were dangerous as well because robbers could roam freely at night in isolated areas.

AT HOME

Most Athenians, whether they were in the city or the country, lived in small homes with two or three rooms. Cooking fires were usually started outside in a portable charcoal or wood stove, then brought in when the fire was hot with less smoke.

Smoke was vented through a small hole in the roof. The roof could also provide a quick way out for the home's occupant if, for example, a debt collector came to the door. And on hot nights, people often slept outdoors on their roofs.

No large or grand homes have been found in ancient Athens, although they have been found in northern Greece and on Delos. Athens's wealthier classes did live in pleasant homes that had perhaps several rooms and an inner courtyard, and some owned both country and city houses. A house unearthed at Dystus on the large island of Euboea has two stories. On the first floor is a large hall next to the open courtyard, which may have had grapevines and fig trees.

During the day, the women—the wife, daughters, and female servants or slaves—worked on weaving and spinning for the family's clothing. Most likely they did this in the open-doored hall or the courtyard, since the weather was often warm. In the evenings, the husband may have entertained his friends in the hall while his wife stayed in an upstairs room.

Most larger homes had women's quarters, where the female head of the household spent much of her time with her children when they were young. These quarters were often guarded by a slave to make sure no strangers entered them.

Tapestries (pieces of thick fabric with designs or pictures woven into them) or embroidered cloth might have decorated the walls. Furniture was fairly simple. To dine, men lay on couches and women sat in chairs. Each person ate from a lightweight table that could be pushed under a couch when not in use. Couches were also used as beds at night. There might also be various stools or chairs and baby- or child-size beds.

Most people did not have a bath at home. But there were baths at the gymnasiums and the number of heated public baths in Athens increased during the fifth century B.C.E. Daily bathing or swimming in the sea was common among the Greeks. Pisistratus, the army commander who ruled Athens in the mid-500s B.C.E., had fountains installed in Athens that were a source of fresh drinking water. When the spout was raised they could also be used for showering.

A MAN'S LIFE IN THE CITY

Wealthy Greek men who did not have to work had the best of what life could offer in ancient Greece. They had slaves to work their country property while they lived in town and wives to run their household. They had children to look after them in old age and make sure they had a proper funeral. They had friends to meet at the agora, the barbershop, or the gymnasium to discuss politics or gossip. They had an education that enabled them to enjoy the newest literature and drama, and few social restrictions placed on their time or where they could go. They had the most time to devote to politics, which was the only proper "occupation" (unpaid) for their status level.

Aristocratic men spent hours at the gymnasium, keeping fit between time spent in the military (they were eligible until age 60). Gymnasiums also served as important social centers where men dis-

Symposia were evening parties for Greek men. Scenes from a symposium were popular subjects for painted drinking cups like this one. Here, a young man lies on a couch while a girl dances to entertain him.

cussed politics and made business deals. A good father would arrange for his son's membership in the best gymnasium, so he would have a better chance of making influential friends. Sometimes the gymnasiums also developed into philosophical or intellectual centers, such as Plato's Academy and Aristotle's Lyceum.

A regular outing for elite Greek males was the symposium. This was an evening drinking party held at someone's home. The symposium was for men only, although female musicians or dancers, most likely slaves, often provided entertainment. The night could be rowdy, or it could offer opportunities to socialize, discuss philosophy, and network.

Men rarely, if ever, socialized with women in the way they did with male friends. One exception to that rule was Pericles' witty, intelligent mistress (*not* his wife) Aspasia (ca. 470–410 B.C.E.). She often accompanied him to symposia (the plural of symposium). Symposia are still held today, although in a much different form. They have changed from rowdy parties to public events focused on discussing important issues.

Ideally, an older, married man formed a close friendship with a young, unmarried man and served as his mentor. Sometimes this relationship was also sexual. In general, the Greeks considered homosexuality a way to encourage teamwork and friendship, especially in the military. A typical Athenian teen, as he entered manhood, would usually end this aspect of his relationship with his mentor and get married. But some men continued their relationship, and two men might form a lifelong partnership. However, such men were also expected to have wives and children.

There was a code of excellence that all men were supposed follow. Odysseus, the hero of Homer's poem the *Odyssey*, was one legendary example. Odysseus was a farmer king. He used his strength, intelligence, and good relationship with the gods to help defeat Troy and then return home after two decades, despite many hardships and adventures along the way.

His wife, Penelope, represented the ideal woman. She was beautiful and faithful to a husband who was gone for 20 years, and she continued to expertly manage their kingdom and their estate.

THE LIVES OF WOMEN

Women did not enjoy high status in Greek society. They could not participate in, or even attend, meetings of the Assembly, for example. They did not engage in cultural activities or go to the gymnasium. Most did not go to school.

Although Greek women had far fewer rights than men, women citizens had broader rights and higher status than *metics* or slaves. A citizen woman could use the court system to address legal issues, such as property disputes, although a man had to represent her in court.

Xenophon gives a glimpse into the role of wealthy women and how they were viewed by their male "guardians" in *Oeconomicus.* This work was written as a dialogue between Socrates and his 30-year-old Athenian friend Ischomachus. It served as a handbook for how to run a household.

In *Oeconomicus*, Ischomachus explains to Socrates his belief that "the gods, from the very beginning, designed the nature of woman for the indoor work and concerns and the nature of man for the outdoor work" (as quoted by Sarah B. Pomeroy and her co-authors in *Ancient Greece*).

Although *Oeconomicus* described the life of a wealthy woman, it still reflects the ideals of Greek society. A Greek housewife ran all aspects of her home. She supervised slaves and servants and cared for them when they were ill. She saw to it that food was properly stored and prepared, and that the amount of food used did not exceed the amount budgeted. She was usually the family member who kept up with religious observances, and she managed the household accounts. She was also responsible for the family's clothing, including making and mending it.

At one point, Ischomachus's wife appears with her face covered with white makeup and wearing high-heeled shoes. Ischomachus gently informs her that he finds her natural beauty and height much more attractive. He tries to make sure she appreciates the importance and elegance of an orderly household. This includes small details such as arranging pots and pans neatly and placing the vases in a good light.

The Goddesses of Greece

The social and legal inequality of women in ancient Greece presented a sharp contrast to the image of some females in Greek mythology. Zeus, a male, may have been the supreme god, but his wife, Hera, and some of his daughters—such as Artemis and Athena—also had great power. They could also torment men who angered them. Hera could not stop her husband from having affairs with mortal women, but she did make life difficult for some of the children he produced with these mistresses. For example, she tried—but failed—to kill Zeus's son Heracles. Artemis, the goddess of hunting, sometimes attacked men who disturbed her or her followers.

The ancient Greeks also wrote about a society of women warriors called Amazons. In some stories they were said to live apart from men. Other stories said they fought alongside the Greeks against common enemies. Once considered mythical, archaeologists are now finding evidence that suggests women warriors may have lived thousands of years ago in Scythia (near the Black Sea). They found graves of women that include weapons. These women may have been the inspiration for the stories of the Amazons. Today, the word *amazon* is used to describe any strong and tall or warlike woman.

The wife of a wealthy citizen spent much of her time indoors at home, although she might participate in a variety of festivals and had a prominent role in family funerals. Sometimes she'd visit with other married women. Her husband or a servant did the shopping at the market, but she might occasionally go to a shop for something personal, such as new pair of shoes. She oversaw the rearing of her children, with the help of servants.

In general, the wealthier a woman was, the less time she spent outside the home. However, most Greek families, citizen or *metic*, were not wealthy, and their female members could not afford to spend their days at home. Those women might work in the agora selling bread or perfume. Citizen women worked alongside *metics* and slave women, none of whom enjoyed any social status.

As a girl growing up and then as a young wife, a woman passed from the guardianship of her father or another male relative to her husband. Marriages were arranged. Girls were usually about 15 or 16 years old, while men were often close to 30. Sometimes fathers arranged a very young daughter's marriage years before the wedding actually took place.

The primary objective in marriage, especially among the wealthy, was to produce successors. It was feared that women with too much freedom and too little attachment to their arranged marriages would have affairs and get pregnant. In fact, it was seen as important for all women to have children. Greek society had a high infant mortality rate—that is, a large number of babies born did not survive into adulthood. So having babies was seen as a key part of a woman's role.

GREEK CHILDREN

Generally speaking, large families were not common in ancient Greece. Poorer families worried about supporting too many children. Families with money were careful not to split their wealth among too many children. Hesiod advised, "Try, if you can, to have an only son to care for the family inheritance: that is the way wealth multiplies in one's halls" (quoted in Robert Flaceliere's *Daily Life in Greece at the Time of Pericles*).

A couple of centuries later, Plato similarly advised couples to have just one son and one daughter. To limit family size, women had abortions or couples left unwanted newborns outside to die or be "rescued." Such children might be raised as slaves or, if they were lucky, raised by a childless couple as their own.

Children were looked to as future providers and caretakers for their parents, and as the ones who would make sure they had a proper funeral. But the Greeks did not see children as merely an economic benefit. Judging from the number of toys that have been unearthed by archaeologists, children were treasured by their ancient Greek parents.

A child's early years were spent at home learning about Greek culture through myths and fables. There were toys to play with: wagons or chariots on wheels that could be pulled by a string, or clay dolls with jointed arms and legs. Children also kept dogs and other animals as pets.

Education from private teachers or schools was available for wealthier families' sons. Boys learned to read and write, solve math problems with an abacus (a frame with beads that was used for counting), play a musical instrument, and sing. Physical training for future military life was begun at about age 12 (except in Sparta). Boys also took part in sporting events at the

Greek children had many types of toys, including terra cotta dolls like this one. This doll has jointed legs; that is, the legs can move separately from the body. Children also played with small wagons, chariots, and small bones used to play a game like jacks.

Fables for the Ages

The plodding tortoise who defeats the over-confident hare, the wolf who dresses as a sheep to catch a tasty meal, the fox who is sure the grapes he cannot reach must be sour—these well-known stories and countless others trace their roots to ancient Greece and a writer named Aesop. Each fable has a moral—a short saying that sums up the point of the story and offers advice for readers to follow.

Some historians think Aesop was a legendary figure of the sixth century B.C.E., not a real author, and the stories credited to him were actually folk tales told orally for generations. Other sources say he was a freed slave from Thrace who may have originally come from North Africa. Some of Aesop's fables were written down around the third century B.C.E., and Roman writers began translating them into Latin during the first century C.E. In modern times, Aesop's fables have appeared in picture books and been turned into cartoons.

THE HEN AND THE GOLDEN EGGS

A farmer and his wife had a hen that laid a golden egg every day. They supposed that the hen must contain a great lump of gold in its inside, and in order to get the gold they killed it. Having done so, they found to their surprise that the hen was no different from their other hens. The foolish pair, thus hoping to become rich all at once, deprived themselves of the gain of which they were assured day by day.

(Source: *Aesop's Fables*. Translated by George Fyler Townsend. Available online. The Internet Classics Archive. URL: http://classics.mit.edu/Aesop/fab.html. Accessed April 29, 2008.)

palaistra, a school devoted to physical education. They practiced such sports as wrestling, boxing, and throwing the javelin (a light spear).

Girls from wealthy families remained at home, but they might receive some basic education in preparation for running their own household. Poor girls learned from their mothers or other female relatives the skills they needed to farm or manage a household. A woman's husband might also continue her education.

Young girls were most visible in public at festivals. Every fourth year, for example, specially honored girls wove a new robe for the huge statue of Athena in the Parthenon. Girls might also be part of a choral performance.

Learning to read and write the Greek language was challenging, because there was no punctuation or even spaces between words. Once a boy knew how to read and write, he began memorizing poetry—especially Homer's stories, which were considered essential knowledge.

Poorer boys and girls would learn a trade and perhaps learn some reading or writing as a result. But most did not have the time or money to learn how to read, so oral learning, through stories, speeches, and songs, remained the way most ancient Greeks came to know about their history and current events.

In general, the Athenians valued education that stressed following traditions and maintaining social order.

COUNTRY LIFE

The urban accomplishments of ancient Greece—the Parthenon, the theater, government, schools of philosophy—are the most famous reminders of ancient Greece. But it is estimated that as much as 80 percent of the Greek population lived outside the cities. They produced the food that was consumed by city dwellers and that helped drive the trade the Greeks had with other countries. The Greeks knew they depended on peasant farmers for their food, so festivals were often planned to accommodate the farmers' busiest seasons.

The ancient Greeks became skilled at terracing the hillsides to create more area to farm. Agricultural terraces are built along the sides of hills. Rocks are used to create terrace steps along the hillsides, and then these steps are filled with soil.

Although the water supplies in Attica were scarce and the soil was thin and rocky, farmers could still grow olives and grapes for wine. In between the rows of olive trees, Athenian farmers planted barley for their *oikos*. Athens had to import most of its grain, but this was not common among the other Greek city-states.

Goats and sheep provided milk and wool for weaving fabric, although sheep's wool was much more common for clothing. Manure was collected for fertilizer, and manure-producing animals also provided food. Bees were kept for honey.

The country farmer and his wife might work alongside two or three slaves. The farmer perhaps kept his hoplite equipment stored in his home or displayed over the fireplace. The *deme* was their center, functioning like a small village. The farmer participated in the government of the *deme* as well as in the government of the polis.

Agricultural life could be unpredictable, and droughts or crop failures pushed farmers into slavery before Solon banned this practice

Terra cotta figures of oxen and a plowman show how the Greeks tended their many crops. About 80 percent of Greeks lived outside the cities and grew food for themselves and the people in urban areas.

in the early sixth century B.C.E.. Still, the farm life was often praised as the ideal way to live. Aristophanes, whose plays urged peace during the Peloponnesian War, wrote of a farmer who fled behind the Athenian walls for safety, but "gaze[d] out towards the country, yearning for peace, sick of the town, missing my own village. . . ." (quoted by Robert Flaceliere in *Daily Life in Greece at the Time of Pericles*).

SPARTAN SOCIETY

Spartan society changed considerably after the two Messenian Wars of the late 700s and the mid-600s B.C.E. The wars left the Messenian people completely under the control of Sparta. Spartan male citizens no longer farmed their own land or manufactured any items for sale or trade. From the 600s B.C.E. on, the Spartans' Messenian serfs, the helots, farmed their own and the Spartans' land and had to hand over most of the food they produced to the Spartans.

Since the helots outnumbered the Spartans and often rebelled against them, Sparta became a strictly military society. Confident in the capabilities of its military, Sparta, unlike most ancient cities, had no walls around it.

Under the social system that developed after the defeat of the Messenians, Spartan male citizens were forbidden by law to perform any type of work except warfare. Female citizens could only raise future hoplites or future mothers of future hoplites. All contributions from Sparta to the literature and art of Greece stopped. Individuality was almost completely suppressed. Both simple and crucial decisions—from what hairstyle to wear to when to get married—were decided by the state.

IN THEIR OWN WORDS

The Women of Sparta

Like so many Greeks, the philosopher Aristotle was horrified at how much freedom Spartan women had. He concluded, incorrectly, that it was because Spartan women refused to be controlled by the laws of their city-state. He could not imagine that the Spartans would actually choose to allow their women to lead freer lives. He also concluded, also incorrectly, that this freedom made Spartan women useless, disorderly, and greedy. In fact, Spartan women, like Spartan men, were strong, brave, and lived simple lives of obedience to the state. In fact, Aristotle's words are more revealing for what they say about Greek men than for what they say about Spartan women.

[A]mong the Spartans in the days of their greatness, many things were managed by their women. But what difference does it make whether women rule, or the rulers are ruled by women? The result is the same. Even in regard to courage, which is of no use in daily life, and is needed only in war, the influence of the Spartan women has been most mischievous. . . . This license of the Spartan women existed from the earliest times, and was only what might be expected. For, during the wars of the Spartans . . . the men were long away from home, and, on the return of peace, they gave themselves into the legislator's hand, already prepared by the discipline of a soldier's life (in which there are many elements of virtue), to receive his enactments. But, when Lycurgus, as tradition says, wanted to bring the women under his laws, they resisted, and he gave up the attempt. . . .

(Source: Aristotle, *The Politics of Aristotle,* Book 2. Translated by Benjamin Jowett. Available online. "Aristotle: Spartan Women," Ancient History Sourcebook. URL: http://www.fordham.edu/halsall/ancient/aristotle-spartanwomen.html. Accessed March 30, 2008.)

This bronze figure of a running Spartan girl from about 600 B.C.E. was probably an ornament or decoration on a larger vessel. Spartan girls and women enjoyed much more freedom than other women in Greece. For example, they were free to play and exercise outdoors, which was not allowed for women in other parts of Greece.

There was little obvious show of wealth among Spartan citizens. Each citizen husband and wife received similar amounts of food, with financial equality among all citizens being the ideal. In reality, however, incomes and wealth did vary within Spartan society, and Aristotle wrote in his *Politics* that poor *ephors* were easier to bribe.

In general, Sparta did not welcome foreigners. It did allow various neighboring peoples, called *perioikoi*, to keep their independence but required them to pay taxes and fight in the Spartan army. The *perioikoi* also performed much of the commercial work that was forbidden to Spartan citizens.

Spartan women enjoyed considerably more freedom than other ancient Greek women. Spartan men spent little time at home, so wives and daughters did not have to take care of their needs. In addition, helots did all manual labor in homes and in the fields.

All these factors meant Spartan women did not have many demands on their time. They could also own property, which most Greek women could not, except in rare circumstances. Spartan women freely exercised outdoors and had a reputation for talking back to their husbands and male relatives.

Spartan children belonged to the state. Boys left home at age seven to live in all-male barracks and begin their training as future hoplites and citizens. The Spartans placed little value on knowledge of literature and music, unless it was for military purposes. Instead, they concentrated on teaching discipline, loyalty, and endurance.

Unlike sheltered Athenian girls, who rarely left their homes, Spartan girls played outdoors, running, wrestling, and wearing very little clothing, like the boys. The idea was to raise strong young women who would bear healthy sons.

By age 12, Spartan boys had learned to march in bare feet. They were given little to eat so they would learn resourcefulness, including how to steal food. They also learned how to kill. By this age, boys also were introduced to an older male mentor and tutor.

WHAT THEY ATE

Most Greeks ate simply. Bread was the main part of every meal. In general, there were two types of bread available at the market: *maza* was made from roasted barley meal kneaded with honey and water or oil and cooked over heat; *artos* was a round wheat loaf baked in an oven. *Maza* was less expensive and so was more common among poorer residents.

Everything else accompanying the bread was referred to as *opson*, whether it was vegetables, olives, eggs, or meat. Vegetables were more expensive than lentils, so lentils were another staple food for the poor. Lentil soup made an inexpensive but filling meal.

A typical Athenian breakfast (one of perhaps two daily meals) was *maza* or *artos* soaked in diluted wine with a few olives or figs. (Wine diluted with water was a regular part of the Athenian diet.)

Meat was usually eaten only at festivals, after a sacrifice. Greeks ate perhaps four pounds of red meat per person each year, plus snails, fish, and birds. People who lived in the country had more meat in their diet, while city dwellers ate more fish, imported from the Black Sea. A

CONNECTIONS

The Importance of Olives

The first harvest from an olive tree represents a long-awaited investment: It takes about a dozen years before a first crop is produced, and another 25 before the tree is fully mature. But then an olive tree can last for centuries.

Olive oil was used by the Greeks to light their lamps, for lubrication, and even on their bodies: Athletes rubbed it on themselves before exercising. Afterward, they used a tool called a *strigil* to scrape off excess oil and dirt before bathing. Greek doctors also used olive oil as a medicine to heal wounds and treat such problems as nausea and insomnia.

The philosopher Democritus (ca. 470–ca. 380 B.C.E.) believed that eating olive oil led to a long life. Modern doctors tend to agree. Olive oil has no cholesterol and is one component of the Mediterranean diet, which also includes vegetables and whole grains. This diet can lower the chances of developing heart disease and cancer, according to a study of more than 20,000 adults in modern-day Greece (as reported in the *New England Journal of Medicine*).

Today, olives remain one of Greece's most important crops. Almost 15 percent of its farmland is devoted to them. The European Union encourages farmers in Greece and several other Mediterranean countries to produce as many olives as possible, and the olives and their oil are then sold outside Europe. This profitable trade has led farmers to abandon the old practice of spacing trees fairly wide apart. Ancient olive groves have been plowed under and new farms, with tightly packed trees, have replaced them. In 2001, the WWF (formerly the World Wildlife Fund) reported that the changes in olive farming were destroying the soil in parts of southern Europe, as well as depriving some animals of their natural habitat.

favorite dish among the Spartans was a broth that included wine, animal blood, and vinegar.

WHAT THEY WORE

Women (or their servants) wove the cloth for the family's clothing. Women usually wore a long dress called a *chiton*. It was made from a large piece of fabric, about 6 feet wide by 11 feet long. The Doric-style *chiton* was actually two dress lengths fastened with a brooch (an ornament with a hinge and a catch, like a pin) at the shoulders. It hung in folds and was belted around the waist. The Ionian style *chiton* had holes cut for the arms and neck and also hung in folds.

The fabric was made from finely woven wool, linen, or cotton muslin. Corinth exported ready-made robes of fine linen.

For warmth women (and men) wore a shawl-like *himation*, which was artfully draped over the shoulders. They also wore caps or veils and carried umbrellas to protect them from the sun. Women wore their long hair up, or sometimes curled, and decorated it with combs made from bone, ivory wood, bronze, or tortoise shell.

Men wore a short tunic. White fabric signified wealth, while others wore natural-colored wool. Spartan children and some poorer Athenians might wear a *himation* alone, just large enough to wrap around the body.

Decorated vases show people of all classes in bare feet, although there were shoemakers. Travelers often wore boots. Wealthy women wore fancy shoes.

THE GODS AND RELIGION

Births, funerals, weddings, the departure of a soldier for war—all were conducted with great attention to rituals intended to please the gods. In both public and private life, religion was an important part of everyday activities.

The gods were believed to be living beings who constantly influenced daily events. Each god had one or two areas of human activity or the physical world that he or she watched over. Poseidon, for example, ruled the seas, while Apollo was the god of both medicine and music. A sailor hoping for smooth waters or a doctor seeking a cure knew which god to pray to for help.

The most important Greek gods and goddesses, 12 in all, were thought to be a family known as the 12 Olympians. They lived atop Mount Olympus in northern Greece, the highest spot in the land.

The gods all traced their roots to Gaia, the "mother Earth" that still lived beneath the Greeks. By feasting on nectar and a special food called ambrosia, the gods could live forever. (Today the word *ambrosia* can be used to describe an especially tasty food that is good enough for the gods.)

The Greek gods were a lot like the Greeks themselves. The gods ate, had relationships and children (sometimes with humans), and argued with one another. Gods could be kindly, cruel, or ridiculous. By creating gods who were just like them, the Greeks made their gods comfortably familiar, even if they were sometimes fearsome.

According to the Greeks' religion, the gods played an active role in the life of humans. Festivals, rituals, sacrifices, and prayers were designed to honor the gods. In return, worshippers expected the gods

A Shine for Shoes

A third century B.C.E. short play by writer Herodas (dates unknown) features two women at a shoe shop arguing with the shoe-maker over the price of his shoes. He lists his fine selection, including "espadrilles, mules, slippers, Ionian bootees, party overshoes, high button-boots . . . Argos sandals, scarlet pumps. . . . " (quoted in Robert Flaceliere's *Daily Life in Greece at the Time of Pericles*).

The Gods and Goddesses of Olympus

The 12 Olympians are not always the same dozen. Some sources do not list Hades because he moved from Mount Olympus to the underworld. Other sources do not include Demeter, who abandoned Olympus when she found out Zeus had allowed Hades to marry her daughter, Persephone, without her permission. This list includes Demeter, for a total of 13 Olympians.

In this list, Leto is a Titan, of the generation of gods who came before the Olympians. Metis is intelligence personified. Maia is the daughter of Atlas, a Titan. Her name means "mother" or "nurse."

NAME	GOD OF	FAMILY ROLE	SYMBOLS
Zeus	Heaven and earth, thunder, all gods and men	Father	Lightning bolt, eagle, oak tree
Hera	Women, childbirth	Zeus's wife (and sister)	Peacock
Poseidon	Seas, earthquakes, horses	Zeus's brother	Trident, dolphin
Hades	The underworld	Zeus's brother	Pomegranates, cap of invisibility

to grant them favors or produce a positive result: victory in war for a city, a good harvest in a particular *deme*, or the birth of a healthy child within an individual family. People also believed the gods could inform them about future events and heal the sick.

The gods' active role in human affairs extended to the physical world. During a storm, the Greeks would say "Zeus rains" or "Zeus thunders," because Zeus was lord of the sky. They literally saw the immortals' footprints in their landscape, as well; they believed a mountaintop got its unusual shape because the winged horse Pegasus stamped his hoof there, and the flat outcrop of the Acropolis was where Athena and Poseidon battled to control Athens.

The Greeks did not have a single organized church that directed how people should worship. Non-religious figures—heads of house-

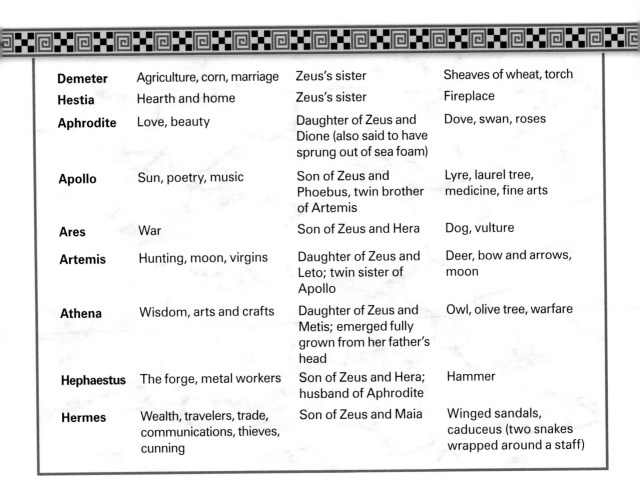

Demeter	Agriculture, corn, marriage	Zeus's sister	Sheaves of wheat, torch
Hestia	Hearth and home	Zeus's sister	Fireplace
Aphrodite	Love, beauty	Daughter of Zeus and Dione (also said to have sprung out of sea foam)	Dove, swan, roses
Apollo	Sun, poetry, music	Son of Zeus and Phoebus, twin brother of Artemis	Lyre, laurel tree, medicine, fine arts
Ares	War	Son of Zeus and Hera	Dog, vulture
Artemis	Hunting, moon, virgins	Daughter of Zeus and Leto; twin sister of Apollo	Deer, bow and arrows, moon
Athena	Wisdom, arts and crafts	Daughter of Zeus and Metis; emerged fully grown from her father's head	Owl, olive tree, warfare
Hephaestus	The forge, metal workers	Son of Zeus and Hera; husband of Aphrodite	Hammer
Hermes	Wealth, travelers, trade, communications, thieves, cunning	Son of Zeus and Maia	Winged sandals, caduceus (two snakes wrapped around a staff)

holds, kings, public officials—led many religious rituals. The Greek religion lacked dogma—a set of strict beliefs and rules. Instead, as long as people stuck to their age-old rituals and did not reject the gods altogether, they could interpret the gods as they wished. That freedom led to less-than-flattering and even comical portrayals of the gods in myth and drama.

The lack of dogma and a highly structured religion also gave Greece's great thinkers the freedom to inquire about the nature of the universe without worrying that their ideas would offend any religious leaders.

The only people who were thought to have direct contact with the gods, writes Robert Parker in *The Oxford History of Greece and the Hellenistic World*, were seers—people who could look into the future. But even these prophets could be ignored without risking serious harm to the community. "The seer knows," Parker writes, "but the ruler decides."

FAMILY RITUALS

Religion played an important role in family events. Weddings often occurred in Gamelion, the month that was considered sacred to Hera, the goddess who oversaw marriage. (Gamelion is roughly equivalent to our January. The Athenian calendar had 10 months of 35 or 36 days each.)

The evening before a teen-aged bride left to go to her new husband's home, her family offered sacrifices to several gods, including Zeus, Hera, and Apollo. The bride gave up her childhood toys, such as her dolls, as offerings to the gods. Then she took a ritual bath in water from a special fountain. Her groom also took a ritual bath.

On the wedding day, the homes of both the bride and groom were decorated with olive and laurel leaf garlands (wreaths). The bride's father hosted a sacrifice and a banquet at which men and women sat separately. The bride was present but wore a veil. She was dressed in her best clothing and wore a garland on her head. Sesame cakes were included in the wedding feast to ensure fertility (the ability to have offspring).

After the meal the bride received her gifts, which often included jewels. At the end of the day, a procession formed to accompany the bride to her new home. Spartan brides were carried off as if they were being kidnapped.

Greek marriages, especially among the wealthy, were primarily a social institution, not a personal relationship. Their purpose was to produce children to be caretakers for their parents in later years and then to inherit the family property. In many cases, wives and husbands did not have much to do with each other once two or three children were born.

In Sparta, men spent little time at home. Marriage was mandatory, but husbands continued to dine with the other men in their communal mess halls. Divorce was legal among the ancient Greeks, but a woman could not set up her own household. She would have to return to the legal protection of a male relative if she wanted to leave her husband.

Weddings in ancient Greece included many rituals, such as this banquet scene from 200 B.C.E. On the wedding day, the bride's father hosted a sacrifice and a banquet at which men and women sat separately.

When a baby was born, an olive branch was hung on the family's front door to announce a boy, or a piece of woolen cloth for a girl. Several days after a child's birth, a ceremony took place to welcome the child into the family and purify the mother and those who had attended her in childbirth. Purification rituals were mandatory after a birth, to cleanse those involved from the "contamination" of childbirth. On the 10th day after a child was born, a banquet was held and the child received a name and gifts.

In Sparta, babies were considered state property. All newborns were shown to local elders—men with some degree of social authority. According to the Roman historian Plutarch (ca. 46–ca. 120 C.E.), the elders examined the baby. If he or she was "well-formed and lusty they allowed it to be reared, but if it was sickly or misshapen they had it taken to the place called Apothetai, a high cliff . . ." where it was abandoned (as quoted in Robert Flaceliere's *Daily Life in Greece at the Time of Pericles*). Unlike other babies of that era, who were wrapped in tight swaddling cloths that restricted their movement,

Spartan babies were loosely covered; they began their life of exercise immediately.

Most Greeks believed that after they died, their spirits, called *shades*, descended into the underworld of Hades. There they wandered aimlessly, experiencing neither pleasure nor pain. Certain religious groups, however, did talk about an afterlife where souls enjoyed bliss they could only dream about on earth.

In either case, a proper funeral was considered essential. At one point laws were passed in various city-states, particularly in Sparta, prohibiting lavish displays at funerals because it raised envy among poorer people. Athens also banned lavish funerals because showing off was considered undemocratic.

Many valuables have been found by archaeologists that were buried along with the dead. These include coins. Money was sometimes were placed in the mouth of the body to pay for the ferry trip from the land of the living to the underworld, which lay across the mythical River Styx.

PUBLIC FESTIVALS AND RITUALS

Almost any time Greeks congregated as a large, mixed group, it was for a festival honoring a god or goddess. Athens's annual calendar was packed with religious festivals, and they took up almost half the days in a year. Some festivals allowed *metics* and even slaves to participate.

At the heart of a festival was the sacrifice, usually of animals but sometimes grain as well. The purpose of a sacrifice was to please the gods and stay on their good side. Before the sacrifice, thousands of people either watched or participated in the procession that accompanied a herd of cattle. The cattle were led to an outdoor altar at the temple to Athena on the Acropolis. There, priests and priestesses conducted the opening festival rituals on behalf of the community.

Sacrifices were performed outside a temple before the assembled crowd. The animals were butchered and a small portion of the meat was burnt on an altar as an offering to, in this case, Athena. Then the rest of the meat was roasted and distributed among the crowd for a communal feast. Over the next several days, Athena was entertained by contests in choral singing, athletics, and instrumental performances.

Women in ancient Greece played their most visible public role in religion and the festivals honoring the gods. In fact, there was even a festival called Thesmorphoria that was exclusively for women. For three days, they interacted freely, without any men controlling their actions. Women also sang in choruses at weddings and other ceremonies, sometimes after receiving special training. Sappho, the great poet, ran a school for aristocratic girls who hoped to sing in a chorus.

The most important public role women played was as priestesses. Like male priests, priestesses were employed by the city-state to serve in the local god's temple. The job was not full-time and priestesses did not need special skills for their work. The position of priestess did not lead to any special political or economic power, although it might boost the social standing of a woman chosen for the job.

CONNECTIONS

The Modern Olympics

The ancient Olympics of Greece led to the modern Olympic Games, first held in Athens in 1896. The founders of the modern games were inspired by the Greek tradition of calling a temporary peace in any wars taking place when the Olympics were scheduled to begin. The modern Olympics were seen as a way to promote peace among nations.

Today, both winter and summer games are held, featuring hundreds of events in more than 35 sports. Athletes still compete in such Greek sports as running, boxing, and wrestling, and the Summer Olympics still has a pentathlon. In the modern event, men and women shoot, fence (swordplay), swim, compete in horse jumping, and run.

In 2004, the Summer Olympics returned to Athens. The opening ceremony included a pageant that retold the history of ancient and modern Greece, and illustrated Greece's many lasting contributions to modern culture. Some ancient Olympian traditions were revived, such as the medal winners receiving crowns of olive leaves. The marathon race began in Marathon and ended in Athens, and the shotput competition was held in the ancient sporting ground in Olympia, with spectators sitting on the grassy hillsides just as the ancient Greeks did.

Even when Greece is not hosting an Olympics, it plays a central part. Greece always marches into the stadium first during the opening ceremony, no matter where the Games are held. And for both the Summer and Winter Games, a torch is lit in Olympia, using the sun's rays reflected off a mirror. The torch is then brought by relay runners to the site of the Games and used to light the Olympic flame. The Olympic flame traces its roots to the ancient Greek games, when a flame in honor of Zeus burned throughout the event.

One special job for priestesses was serving as a temple's oracle. People came to the oracle seeking advice or information about the future. The priestess of the oracle went into a trance that supposedly enabled her to communicate with the temple's god. She then provided an answer for the questioner. The most famous oracle was at the temple of Apollo at Delphi.

ART AND ATHLETICS IN RELIGION

Religion and its festivals led to important developments in Greek cultural life that have influenced the modern world, as well. The annual Athenian festival honoring Dionysus led to the development of Greek drama. The Greeks first celebrated the god of wine and merrymaking by singing and dancing to praise him. The songs and dances evolved into plays, with first one actor speaking to the crowd, then another, until drama was born. Theaters then appeared across the Greek world.

Music and dance continued to play key roles in Greek drama. Men played all the roles, wearing costumes and masks. Playwrights entered contests to see whose play would be performed, and the winners became some of the ancient world's first celebrities. Actors and producers also won awards for their work.

The festival honoring Zeus at Mount Olympia, held every four years, became known as the Olympics and was the best athletics competition in Greece. Athletics was considered an appropriate way for men to prove their merit and was seen as necessary for military preparedness. Male athletes and spectators arrived from all over the Greek world (women were strictly forbidden to attend). Athletes arrived early to give themselves time to prove to judges they were of Greek birth.

The actual competition was held in an enclosed area called the *altis.* The area included two temples (one dedicated to Zeus and one to his wife, Hera), as well as a stadium. In fact, the English word *stadium* comes from the Greek word *stadion,* a unit of measurement of about 600 feet.

Spectators camped out on the surrounding plains at night, and by day crowded the grassy hillsides overlooking the stadium as runners raced back and forth, rather than around its perimeter. Stones embedded in the ground held special starting gates (the stones are still visible today). Drawings of the games on Greek pottery show referees holding rods to keep eager athletes from jumping the starting signals.

Athletes competed in the pentathlon, a combined contest of long jump, running, discus and javelin throwing, and wrestling. (The name comes from the Greek words *pente*, meaning "five," and *athlon*, "contest.") Other events included foot races of various lengths, horse and chariot races, boxing, and an event called the *pankration*. This sport was a blend of boxing and wrestling. Fighters could inflict pain in any way, except by gouging their opponent's eyes or biting.

All Olympic athletes competed as individuals, rather than as part of a city-state team. And athletes at the Olympic games not only represented physical excellence, they also represented wealth. After all, a top athlete needed plenty of time—*leisure* time—to develop his strength, speed, and agility. A typical Greek peasant farmer had no time to train for athletic competitions.

The award for Olympic champions was quite simple: Winners were crowned with a plain wreath of olive or laurel leaves. But once an athlete returned home, the honors he received could really add up, especially because the games gained in importance over the decades from their beginnings in 776 B.C.E. In fact, the Olympics inspired young men to try to become professional athletes (there were athletic contests at other festivals during the off years of the Olympics). Top athletes could bring in a decent income from appearance fees and by participating in other sporting events, much as they do today.

CHAPTER 6

GREEK ART, PHILOSOPHY, AND SCIENCE

THE GREEKS CREATED A BODY OF LITERATURE AND philosophy whose impact endures into the 21st century. People before the Greeks thought about the nature of the world, but the Greeks left behind a written record that stimulated debate and laid a foundation for future study. Norman Cantor and Peter Klein, in their introduction to *Ancient Thought: Plato and Aristotle*, wrote, "Not only did the Greeks fashion new forms of intellectual artistic expression—tragedy, history, and philosophy—but they provided an entirely new set of intellectual categories through which the world could be viewed and judged."

HOMER AND EARLY LITERATURE

The foundation of ancient Greek culture was the poet Homer. Greeks referred to their favorite storyteller as simply "the poet." Homer's significance was so great that several city-states claimed to be his birthplace. The stories he is credited with brilliantly retelling—the two epic poems *Iliad* and *Odyssey*—had been passed down orally for centuries.

Homer's literature served a variety of purposes. With beautiful language, it spoke to the Greeks of their noble past and of their special relationship with the gods, and it offered a sense of unity that overcame their geographic barriers and political separation. Along with the Bible, Homer's works are considered the basis of literature in the Western world.

The way Homer told the story of the *Iliad*, it is not about the Trojan War as much as it is about "repercussions of the quarrel between the mightiest Greek hero, Achilles, and . . . Agamemnon," wrote Kenneth

OPPOSITE
This vase from about 510 B.C.E. shows a pottery workshop. Pottery was an important export in ancient Greece. Earlier styles from Corinth showed black figures painted on red clay. Later styles from Athens showed unpainted figures on a black background.

J. Atchity in *The Classical Greek Reader.* It is a story about heroes and gods, driven by all-too-human weaknesses and misunderstandings, and it is a myth "by which the Greeks explained . . . all of life and death."

In the *Odyssey*, the hero Odysseus introduces the concept of moral relativism (doing whatever is required at a given moment to survive). This earns him Athena's admiration. "We're both old hands at the arts of intrigue," she tells Odysseus.

The other significant early Greek writer was Hesiod, who worked around 700 B.C.E. He was from Boeotia, an area with rich farmland, and his book *Works and Days* dealt with agricultural life as well as his own philosophy. In it, he discussed the difference between good strife and bad strife. Good strife are those challenging situations, such as competitions, that make us work harder. Bad strife is created by self-centered persons (or the gods) and disrupts social harmony.

POETRY

Sappho (d. ca. 580 B.C.E.), born in Mytilene on the island of Lesbos, is considered one of the first poets to deal with personal thoughts and feelings. She was much admired by ancient Greek writers who followed her, including Plato. Although she was a wife and mother, she often wrote of erotic feelings toward other women. Consequently, members of the medieval Christian Church destroyed much of her poetry.

Pindar (ca. 518–438 B.C.E.) was a Theban aristocrat educated in Athens. His lyric poetry was much in demand. Lyrical poetry was sung to accompaniment of the lyre, a musical instrument much like a small harp. Pindar was the most famous and productive lyric poet of his era.

What survives of his works are four books of victory odes he was commissioned to write for his fellow aristocrats, who were athletic champions. Just as it was not proper for generals to boast of their military accomplishments, Pindar's musical odes did not focus on any one individual's athletic achievements. Rather, they described the athlete's noble family or even told a mythological story related to the champion's success.

THE BIRTH OF DRAMA

Greek drama developed as part of Athens's festival tribute to Dionysus, who was the son of Zeus and a mortal Theban woman. Dionysus was the god of drama and wine. Every year playwrights were chosen to pres-

---

A Poem by Sappho

*In gold sandals
dawn like a thief
fell upon me*

——

(From *The Classical Greek Reader*)

ent their plays at the festival. At first, these were primarily tragedies, but comedies also eventually were presented. The tragedies were written in verse and drew heavily on Greek mythology, featuring stories of often-tragic dealings between humans and gods.

Plays were performed at an outdoor theater each spring. As many as 14,000 spectators might crowd onto the Acropolis hillside that served as theater seating. By the fifth century B.C.E., stone seats had been added to the hillside.

The stage was a raised platform and scenery was often simple, but the actors' costumes were elaborate. There might even be special effects, such as an actor being lifted by a crane to appear to fly. The

Classic Tragedy

This excerpt is from Sophocles' great tragic play, *Antigone*. After King Oedipus was exiled from the city of Thebes, his younger son Eteocles claimed that he should be king. He sent away his older brother, Polyneices. Polyneices then attacked Thebes, but neither son won because they killed each other in battle. The new Theban king, Creon, declared that Eteocles would be buried and honored as a hero while Polyneices' body would not be buried, and would be left to rot. The penalty for trying to bury the body was death.

Polyneices' sister Antigone insisted that her brother's body must be buried so that his spirit can rest in peace. She went to the battlefield and performed the burial rituals over Polyneices' body. Then she allowed herself to be captured. A defiant Antigone was brought to Creon, who demanded to know how she dared to break his law. Antigone insisted that even if her actions went against Creon's commands, they did not break the higher laws of the gods. Her impassioned speech concludes by insulting Creon and his laws.

I know all too well I'm going to die—how could I not?—it makes no difference what you decree. And if I have to die before my time, well, I count that a gain. When someone has to live the way I do, surrounded by so many evil things, how can she fail to find a benefit in death? And so for me meeting this fate won't bring any pain. But if I'd allowed my own mother's dead son to just lie there, an unburied corpse, then I'd feel distress. What going on here does not hurt me at all. If you think what I'm doing now is stupid, perhaps I'm being charged with foolishness by someone who's a fool.

(Source: Sophocles, *Antigone*. Translated by Ian Johnston, Arlington, Va.: Richer Resources Publications, 2005.)

playwright was the show's director, producer, and songwriter, too, because the dramatic storyline was enhanced by singing parts performed by a chorus.

The first Greek plays had just a single actor and a chorus, with the main emphasis still on singing and dancing. Aristotle credited Aeschylus (525–456 B.C.E.), an aristocrat from Eleusis in Attica, with creating the type of performance that is familiar to theatergoers even today. Aeschylus added a second actor and minimized the role of the chorus in his work. Like most men of his time, Aeschylus fought in the Greek-Persian Wars; in fact, his brother Cynegirus was killed at Marathon.

Aeschylus wrote more than 70 plays, including *Seven Against Thebes*, which inspired classic films such as *The Seven Samurai* and *The Magnificent Seven*. He won many Dionysian festival competitions, but he was defeated in 468 B.C.E. by the 27-year-old Sophocles (ca. 496–406 B.C.E.). Sophocles' plays introduced a third and later a fourth actor, expanding the importance and variety of dialogue in drama.

Euripides (480–406 B.C.E.) was another great Greek dramatist. His plays often featured strong female roles. One example is *Medea*, the story of a non-Greek woman from the kingdom of Colchis who was considered a witch. She and the Greek prince Jason have had two sons together. But then Jason plans to marry a Corinthian princess for the prestige it will bring him. Medea eventually murders Jason's bride-to-be, and then their children. Yet Euripides presents her—an "uncivilized foreigner"—as a sympathetic character driven to despair and rage by the cold and smug Greek Jason.

COMEDY

Originally, the purpose of comedy was to critique politics, government, or society in a humorous way—the humor making the criticism easier to swallow. This particular kind of comedy is called *satire*. Aristophanes was the greatest of the Classical Greek comic playwrights. He used humor to express his views on a number of social issues, including his desire for peace during Athens's darkest hour—the Peloponnesian War. He also made fun of Athens's leader Cleon, the philosopher Socrates, and even Dionysus, who was portrayed as a coward in *The Frogs*—which was being performed at the festival honoring Dionysus! Aristophanes wrote 40 plays, of which 11 survive. The humor in his plays ranged from slapstick to obscene to sophisticated and sharp.

CONNECTIONS

Modern Theater and the Greeks

Both the form and content of ancient Greek theater survive today. In addition, the modern English words for the two main styles of drama, *tragedy* and *comedy*, come from the Greek words *tragoidia* and *komoidia*.

Aristotle studied the works of the great tragic writers and described the structure he found in his *Poetics*. He believed the plot of a play should focus on one main theme and take place over just one day. From Aristotle's writings, later playwrights came up with the idea of the "three unities" of place, time, and action: A play should be set in one location, unfold over a limited time frame (no more than one day), and focus on just one major event. Aristotle also said the purpose of dramatic tragedy is to stir fear and pity in the audience, leading to an emotional release called *catharsis*.

The three unities were held up as an ideal for centuries and are still taught today, although many playwrights do not follow them. Students of theater also learn about catharsis and the role drama plays in creating an emotional tension in the audience that is released by the ending.

The plays Aristotle studied are still performed around the world. The great Greek playwrights wrote about themes that all humans understand: love, family rivalries, revenge, suffering, the horror of war.

A new style of comedy developed during the fourth century B.C.E. This new comedy eliminated satire and the chorus. It used actors to tell simple stories of people in real-life situations. Certain character types—what are called stock characters—appeared in every play. These usually included a young woman and the man who pursued her.

The best-known writer of new comedy style was Menander (ca. 342–292 B.C.E.). Aristotle and other ancient Greeks noted that Menander was not a particularly funny comic writer. But other playwrights praised his ability to write dialogue and show a more realistic version of life.

The key feature of new comedy was that it was not political. This is partly because Menander wrote while Athens was under Macedonian occupation, and political criticism could lead to trouble. However, while new comedy was more realistic, it still did not show real life. Menander's plays were more like television shows now—based on real life, but not realistic.

Menander's greatest importance came as an influence on later Roman playwrights, such as Plautus (ca. 254–184 B.C.E.). Plautus took the stock characters and situations from Athenian new comedy and added gags, puns, and physical humor. His style has influenced play-wrights and comedians right up to the present day. The musical *A Funny Thing Happened on the Way to the Forum* is based on Plautus's work, using some of the same jokes that cracked up Roman audiences more than 2,000 years ago.

RECORDING HISTORY

Another important Greek innovation in ancient literature was record-ing true events—history. (The word comes from the Greek *istorie*, which means "inquiry" or "research"). The Roman statesman Cicero (106–43 B.C.E.) called Herodotus the father of history for his books about the Persian wars, which were based on actual events and person-alities—unlike Homer's *Iliad*.

Herodotus's interests went beyond Greece, and his *Histories* include curious facts about other cultures. Much of what we know today about the history of the Greek world and its neighbors comes from Herodotus. However, since his descriptions were often based on how Greeks imagined life to be rather than reality, modern historians understand his accounts are not always accurate.

Herodotus's competitor was Thucydides, whose subject, the Pelo-ponnesian War, was personally familiar to him. He began record-ing events when the war first broke out, immediately recognizing its importance. He also added analysis and drew his own conclusions about events. He wrote in his books that he based his opinions both on what he saw and on what other eyewitnesses to events told him.

Other Greek historians who followed Herodotus and Thucydides included Xenophon. Like Thucydides, Xenophon was exiled from Athens and his history was therefore sympathetic to Sparta. Another historian was Polybius (ca. 205–ca. 125 B.C.E.), who wrote about the transition of the Greek world to Roman rule.

Modern historians value the ancient Greek historians for their eyewitness accounts and insights into social and political attitudes. Yet modern readers cannot take the ancient histories as absolute truth. In some cases, the historians relied on oral sources, which might have included legends along with facts. The Greek writers also brought their own opinions to what they wrote, choosing to include or exclude cer-tain facts as they saw fit (modern historians struggle with this same

IN THEIR OWN WORDS

History or Just a Story?

In *The Histories*, Herodotus described the conflict between the Greeks and the Persian Empire. While telling the story of their own civilization in conflict with another, many people would be inclined to take sides. But Herodotus tried to show each side's perspective in the struggle.

Herodotus also carefully recorded the customs of many peoples and countries. Often this information was gathered from people he met, rather than from seeing things himself. He tried to evaluate the truth of the information he received, and sometimes offered it with a caution that it might not be accurate. Still, modern historians believe not all of Herodotus's information was accurate. This is part of his description of the people of Thrace, a region north and east of Greece.

They consider tattooing a mark of high birth, the lack of it a mark of low birth. The best man, in their opinion, is the idle man, and the sort least worthy of consideration is the agricultural laborer. The most reputable sources of income are war and plunder. So much for their striking customs.

The only deities they worship are Ares, Dionysus, and Artemis—though their kings, in contrast to people generally, pay particular reverence to Hermes; they swear by no other deity but Hermes, and claim their own descent from him.

When a rich Thracian is buried, the custom is to lay out the body for three days, during which, after a preliminary period of mourning, a feast is held of all sorts of animals slaughtered for the purpose. Then the body is buried, with or without cremation, a mound is raised over it, and elaborate games set on foot. The most valuable prizes in the games are awarded for single combat.

(Source: Herodotus, *The Histories*. Translated by Aubery de Selincourt. London: Penguin Classics, 2003.)

issue). Still, as both literature and history, the Greek texts remain entertaining and useful.

MUSIC

Music was indispensable to the Greeks. The god Hermes was credited with making the first lyre from a tortoiseshell when he was an infant. Music was recommended by Plato as a standard part of a child's education, and in the *Iliad* Achilles was as skilled with his lyre as he was with his weapons.

This drinking cup shows two muses; the one on the right carries a lyre, a type of small harp. Music was a vital part of Greek culture, and it was a standard part of every Greek child's education.

The works of poets were often regarded as songs, and by the sixth century B.C.E., the performance of poetry was generally accompanied by a lyre. The simpler form of the lyre could be found in Greek homes, while a similar and more complex instrument, the *kithara*, was played by professional musicians at festival competitions.

Another type of festival performance was the *dithyramb*, a dancing chorus that evolved into drama. The word *orchestra* comes from the Greek word for "dance" (*orcheisthai*), and referred to the round stage where the chorus members performed.

The *aulos*, a reed instrument (like an oboe or a clarinet) that often had two pipes, was also popular and was often used to play dancing music. But lyre playing was especially desirable because the performer could sing and play at the same time.

POTTERY AS ART AND HISTORY

The masks worn by the actors in Greek tragedies and comedies were quite large. They had exaggerated expressions, so audience members who were seated some distance from the stage could see them. One reason we know this is from the detailed decorations on Athenian pottery. The subjects of these decorations could be anything from mythological stories to household scenes to country farms.

Another popular art form in ancient Greece was wall painting. Although none of those works survives, we can get an idea of what the wall art looked like from copies painted onto pottery. Most of the pottery that survived the centuries unbroken has been found in tombs.

Playing the Oldies

It is not so difficult to put on an ancient Greek drama; many of the works by Greece's top playwrights have been copied and preserved. But it is not so easy to replicate a musical concert, using reproductions of ancient instruments. But an Australian musicologist is playing musical detective to figure out what Greek music must have been like.

Michael Atherton, a professor at the University of Western Sydney, is one of the people who studies clues about music in ancient Greece and then tries to reproduce the sounds. Although there was no form of written music, some of those clues are contained in musical documents that still exist, though most have missing sections. Other clues include a few fragile and valuable instruments that have survived over the years, some descriptions from sources such as Plato and Aristotle of how different instruments sounded, and pictures of the instruments and how they were held that are painted on ancient pottery. With the help of a violinmaker, Atherton tries to build copies of the Greek instruments and then figures out how to play them.

Corinth was the most prominent producer of Greek pottery in the seventh and eighth centuries B.C.E. The typical Greek style of black figures painted on orange or red clay containers developed in Corinth. Corinthian potters were influenced by Near Eastern styles that featured geometric patterns and animal figures. However, the black figures on Corinthian pottery are not very detailed, and reveal little about the life of their makers.

The clay in Attica contains an element, illite, that gives its pottery glaze a beautiful glow. By the sixth century B.C.E., Athenian pottery was the dominant product and was imitated by the Corinthians. One market-savvy Athenian craftsman, Nicosthenes (d. ca. 505 B.C.E.), made a steady business of selling his work to the Etruscans in Italy by decorating his pottery with popular Etruscan themes, such as boxing and reproductions of scenes from Etruscan artwork. Some pottery was whimsical, such as the cup found in Attica and dated to about 460 B.C.E. that is shaped like a cow's hoof and painted with a scene of a farmer and his cow.

An innovation in Athenian pottery dating from about 525 B.C.E. was the reverse of the Corinthian black figure drawings. Instead, figures or objects were left unpainted but were given detail by etched-in lines, while the background was painted black. These painted pots offered detailed views of life in Athens. Winners of athletic competitions often received as a prize painted vases filled with olive oil from the trees of the sacred grove of Athena in the Academy.

By the fourth century B.C.E., Athens was in decline economically and production of its famous vases died out as the pottery of southern Italy came into fashion. But fortunately, a number of painted vases survive from Athens's most prosperous days, giving historians vividly detailed pictures of ancient Greek life and culture.

SCULPTURE TRANSFORMED

The artwork of the ancient Greeks began on a small scale with intricately carved jewelry. Pieces have been found dating to the 10th and ninth centuries B.C.E. While Greek potters were producing more and more naturalistic images, Greek sculptors were gaining confidence and skill working with stone.

The ancient Greeks considered the first sculptor of note to be Daedalus, whom supposedly lived around 1100 B.C.E. There are many legends about Daedalus, but there is no historical evidence that he actually existed. Even so, modern historians named a style of sculpture featuring small, abstract figures with triangular faces Daedalic in his honor. The unknown artists who made these sculptures were influenced by the art of the Near East.

Sixth-century B.C.E. Greek sculpture looked Egyptian: strait-backed, stylized nude male figures called *kouroi* (the singular is *kouros*) faced forward with arms down at their sides and the left foot slightly in front of the right. A female version was a draped figure, and was usually placed in cemeteries. Eventually, relief sculpture (three-dimensional images that emerge from a flat or curved surface) began to be added to the bases of the *kouroi* statues.

By the fifth century B.C.E., Greek artists and writers were aware that the Greeks were building a

The Greeks developed theater as part of their religious festivals. The forms of tragedy and comedy they created are the basis of all theater, even today. Greek actors usually wore masks like this one, which represents tragedy, to help audiences easily understand what characters they represented.

new political and military force in the world. They wanted to both honor their culture and get away from the foreign models they had once copied. In sculpture, this led to greater realism and the depiction of action, as in the Discobolus ("discus thrower") sculpted by Myron of Eleutherae (ca. 490–430 B.C.E.). Like all of his work, it was cast in bronze, but the only versions of it remaining are Roman copies in marble.

The sculptor Polyclitus (464–420 B.C.E.) spent his long career in Argos, where he ran a school. His sculpture was representative of the Greek admiration for symmetry (being the same on both sides of an imaginary center line) and balance in art or architecture. The Greeks believed symmetry reflected perfection and that humans should imitate it in their art.

Polyclitus and his competitor Phidias (ca. 500–ca. 432 B.C.E.) were the masters during the Classical period of Greek art. The style of Polyclitus fit into a Greek ideal of art that dated back to the *kouros*, of trying to represent the perfect body. Polyclitus began a trend among sculptors. They copied the proportions of his sculpture and began featuring more humans, rather than gods, in their work. Attention to every detail of the subject matter, such as the folds on a cloak, showed the great technical skill developed during this period, and influenced artists for centuries to come.

ARCHITECTURE

The two main styles of architecture in ancient Greece were Doric and Ionic. The Doric style was seen in temples and other public buildings on the Greek mainland. The Ionic style was seen in Ionia and on the islands in the Aegean Sea. Today in architecture, the two styles are called *orders*. The orders are perhaps most easily identified by the types of columns used. Doric columns are wider, sturdier, and more simply styled than the slimmer, more decorative Ionic columns.

A third order, Corinthian, was first used primarily inside temples. It dates from the fifth century B.C.E. Corinthian columns are similar to the ones in the Ionic order, but the tops of the Corinthian columns are more elaborately decorated. Roman architects later popularized the use of the Corinthian order on the outside of buildings. These types of columns are still used today in buildings designed in the Classical style.

The most readily available building materials in ancient Greece were stone and wood. In Corinth, the cultural center of early Archaic Greece, a temple for Poseidon was made entirely of stone. Its walls were

Tricks of the Eye

The Parthenon was designed by two builders, Ictinus (fifth century B.C.E.) and Callicrates (fifth century B.C.E.). They made use of some visual tricks that required great technical skills. For example, columns, when placed perfectly vertical, actually appear to be leaning slightly outward. So the Parthenon's columns were angled slightly inward to appear to be at a 90-degree angle to the ground. Also, to the human eye columns appear to be slightly tapered in the middle, so the actual columns had a slight bulge added to them in the center to compensate. Each column was made from sections, or drums, of marble stacked one atop the other, so each drum had to be cut precisely at slightly different angles, since the entire column had to lean inward. And the images sculpted into the frieze, placed high atop the building, would have been difficult for temple visitors to see, so the top part of the frieze was carved about two inches deeper than the bottom part.

Artist, Architect, Engineer

Daedalus's name means "cunning fabricator." According to ancient Greek history, he was an architect and engineer as well as an artist. The ancient Greeks also credited him with several inventions, including the axe and sails for ships. Modern historians doubt he was a real person, though.

Today Daedalus is known as the main character in several important Greek myths. On the island of Crete, he is said to have built the first labyrinth, a maze of passageways and dead-ends, that contained the Minotaur, a monstrous bull. Daedalus also built a set of wings for himself and his son Icarus, so they could escape Crete after its king imprisoned them. The wings were made of bird feathers and wax. Daedalus instructed his son not too fly to close to sun because the wax would melt. Icarus ignored his father's advice and fell to his death.

then covered with stucco (a type of plaster) and painted with geometric designs and figures.

As Greece grew more prosperous, marble was preferred, despite the higher cost. Athens was fortunate to discover a large source of marble just to the north at Mount Pentelikon. The city-state also had increasing wealth, thanks to money coming in from the Delian League after the Persian Wars and from the Laurium silver mines, so it could afford this expensive material.

Given the ready supply of marble and Athenian wealth, Pericles, the great Athenian leader, was able to establish an extensive public building program. They aim was to show the world that his was city the leader among the Greeks. The biggest and most important new building was the Parthenon, a temple dedicated to Athena (construction of a new temple for the goddess had actually begun during the years of the Persian War, before the destruction of the Acropolis).

Athena's new temple was Doric in style and richly decorated with a 524-foot frieze, or sculpted band, around the top of the building. The frieze featured a single scene: the great procession through Athens that began the Panathenaic festival. The procession is shown moving from two starting points, finally meeting in the center of the eastern side of the building, over the temple's entrance.

The temple also has 92 intricately carved panels called *metopes*, and two carved column pediments, which are triangular pieces between the roof and the columns on the building's front and back. The *metopes* were painted in bright colors and show mythological battles that proclaim the triumph of Greek culture over barbarians (uncivilized people—anyone who was not Greek).

Although today surviving Greek sculptures and buildings are in natural white marble, the ancient Greeks painted their statues and architectural friezes in vivid colors. So the Parthenon was not just an architectural marvel; it also featured an explosion of color. This must have been especially dramatic against the sunny, blue-sky backdrop of southern Greece.

Other new buildings on the Acropolis included the Erechtheum, an irregularly shaped building whose interior honored several gods. There was also the smaller Athena Nike (victory) temple. On its walls was a large painting depicting the victory at Marathon.

Altogether, construction on the Acropolis lasted from about 450 to 405 B.C.E. Historians know about how the buildings were constructed—including what kind of craftsmen were used and how much they were paid—because detailed records engraved in marble have survived. More importantly, the ruins of the whole project survive. "Mighty indeed are the marks and monuments of our empire which we have left," said Pericles of the Acropolis (as quoted by Thucydides and found in *The Cambridge Illustrated History of Ancient Greece*). "Future ages will wonder at us as the present age wonders now."

The buildings erected on the Acropolis and across Greece had a lasting impact on Western architecture. The Romans copied the various orders. They also copied the Greek fondness for grand public buildings that inspired awe for the gods and embodied the Greek values of order and balance.

From the Renaissance through modern times, architects have turned back to these Greek and Roman ideals. (Although they did not copy the Greek and Roman habit of painting their buildings and sculpture. By the time other Europeans saw them, the paint had worn off.) The ancient styles are often used in buildings that are thought to be "temples" to such things as government, academics, and commerce. For example, the U.S. Supreme Court Building in Washington, D.C., with its pediments and Corinthian columns, reveals the importance its occupants play in the American legal system. In New York, the U.S. Stock Exchange is another Greek-temple-like structure. It is famous for the sculpture on its pediment showing Integrity as a woman protecting the inventions of humanity.

Across Europe and North America today, many legislative buildings and parliaments echo the ancient Greco-Roman architectural styles. In this way, they connect the present systems of government to the greatness of Athenian democracy.

Nashville's Parthenon

Today Athens's Parthenon is an ancient ruin. But to get an idea of what the Parthenon might have looked like in its glory days in Athens, head to Nashville, Tennessee. The city of Nashville built a full-scale replica of the Parthenon in 1897 for the 100th anniversary celebration of Tennessee statehood. Surrounded by a large city park, it originally was made of plaster, wood, and brick, but was rebuilt in 1920 of concrete.

THINKING ABOUT THE UNIVERSE

Classical Athens was home to philosophy schools that drew students from all over Greece and, later, the Roman Empire. The great teachers of Athens remain some of the best-known thinkers today: Socrates, Plato, and Aristotle. At their schools, and at others, students learned mathematics, botany, biology, and astronomy, as well as philosophy—the study of human values and knowledge.

But Athens was not where the idea of philosophy began. The first Greek philosophers came from Miletus, a city in Ionia. In the sixth century B.C.E., these thinkers started formally studying questions that humanity had been thinking about for centuries: What is the universe all about and what is the role of humans in it?

Once again, the Greeks were inspired by knowledge they obtained from others—in this case, the Babylonians' advanced knowledge of astronomy. The Babylonians kept detailed records of the movement of stars and planets and could accurately predict their future movements, suggesting the universe had some kind of order. The Greek thinkers, however, were not content to just record what they saw and make predictions. They wanted to understand why the universe worked the way it did. They then also began to ask "why" and "how" about events in the physical world and in the thought processes of humans.

The Greeks' studies were very original, because people had always assumed the answers to these questions were found in religion. It thunders because Zeus is angry, or people should behave a certain way because it pleases the gods. But the first philosophers doubted these divine interpretations of the natural world. They believed they could discover the order of the universe through observation and thought. This belief led to science and philosophy.

Early on, these two fields were closely linked. Philosopher-scientists asked, what is our world and the life in it made of? What is reality and what is perception? The answers to these questions combined scientific theory and observation with creative reasoning.

THE FIRST PHILOSOPHERS

Thales of Miletus (ca. 640–546 B.C.E.) was the first known philosopher. He came up with the theory that water is the essence of life and reality. This was the first time a thinker dismissed the idea that the gods might have something to do with reality, too. He is therefore credited with starting the field of physical science. Among his accomplishments, Thales predicted the solar eclipse of 585 B.C.E.

Anaximander (ca. 610–546 B.C.E.) followed Thales, possibly as his student. He disagreed with Thales' water theory, though, and suggested that the substance of the universe and the life in it is unidentifiable. He also said our world is but one of many.

Anaximander was followed by his student, Anaximenes (ca. 590–525 B.C.E.). He defined his teacher's "unidentifiable substance" as air. He based his idea on his observations of water evaporating—water "changing into air." Even the human soul consists of air, Anaximenes said.

Though their theories might sound overly simple today, these three men from Miletus were quite revolutionary in suggesting that human beings can use their own reasoning and observations to come up with the definition of life itself.

Another great thinker from Ionia was Pythagoras (b. mid-sixth century B.C.E.), although his greatest fame came from work he did after he left his homeland. He believed the universe could be explained through mathematics. He taught that souls were immortal and entered new bodies after people died, and that a person's actions in life influenced what kind of body his or her soul would enter next.

The Ionians were followed in the fifth century B.C.E. by other philosopher-scientists who continued to challenge the ideas of those who came before them about the universe and the nature of reality. Parmenides (b. 510 B.C.E.) was significant for suggesting the universe to be an unchanging, fixed entity, despite what the five senses might claim. His challenge, then, to future philosophers was to use intellectual methods as well as their observations to support their ideas of reality.

Another Ionian, Anaxagoras (ca. 500–428 B.C.E.), said change is inevitable because of minute particles that are in constant motion. These particles, or seeds, made up everything that existed, forming different

CONNECTIONS

The Pythagorean Theorem

The philosopher Pythagoras and his followers did important work in mathematics. Pythagoras is best known today for the theorem that bears his name. Students around the world learn that the sum of the squares of the length of each side of a right triangle (a triangle with one 90-degree angle) equals the square of the length of the hypotenuse (the longest side): $a^2 + b^2 = c^2$. With this formula, a person can determine the length of any side of a right triangle if he or she knows the length of the other two sides.

Fanatic Followers

The philosopher Pythagoras developed what seems today like a religious cult (a small group of people who follow a single leader and reject traditional practices). A group of students, both men and women, lived with him apart from Greek society. The Pythagoreans were vegetarians and avoided the usual Greek religious rituals.

combinations to create such diverse things as people and dogs. His arguments were expanded on by other philosophers, who said these small particles could not be divided into smaller particles. In Greek, these particles were called *atoma*, or "uncuttable." This led to the English words *atom* and *atomic*. Modern science has shown that the Greek atomists were right about the idea of tiny particles that are always in motion and that make up all matter in the universe.

SOCRATES AND PLATO

Socrates (470–399 B.C.E.), an Athenian, is credited with steering philosophy toward the study of morality. In a city that valued beauty and wealth, Socrates was unusual. He came from humble birth and chose to remain poor. He supported his wife and children as a stonemason (someone who cuts and builds with stone) and served Athens as a hoplite.

But Socrates spent his later years wandering through Athens, making it his work to engage citizens in friendly but pointed discussions about justice, courage, and other moral issues. He did not ask for payment from those he taught informally. Perhaps his most famous line, as reported by Plato in his *Apology* (quoted in *The Last Days of Socrates*), is, "The unexamined life is not worth living."

His discussions involved leading his conversation partner through a variety of questions, often arriving at unexpected conclusions. Socrates would claim he did not know the answers to the questions he asked. By asking questions, Socrates forced his listeners to draw their own conclusions, although he was always the one guiding the direction of the argument. This style of teaching is today called the *Socratic method* and is still used, primarily in law schools but also in other fields of study.

Socrates was concerned with questions of right and wrong. This set him apart from a group called the Sophists. These were traveling teachers-for-hire who were specialists in the art of rhetoric. Public speaking was an important skill for Greek aristocrats. One may have wanted to sway Assembly voters on a particular issue, be persuasive in court, or impress other influential men at a symposium.

The Sophists promised to take students beyond rhetoric and teach them how to use logic to turn any argument in their favor. They were especially popular with politicians. But they came under criticism for their tendency to disregard right and wrong in favor of winning arguments.

Death of a Philosopher

Socrates was a good-humored character with a big personality and many influential friends. He was also an original, independent thinker, and this stirred suspicion in many Athenians. They accused him of destroying the morals of the city's youth with his teachings. His critics claimed that he encouraged people to reject the traditional Greek gods and discover new ways of explaining human existence. Although the ancient Greeks had no real religious rules to disobey in the first place, after the Peloponnesian War many Athenians were insecure about their relationship with the gods.

Socrates was a target because of his refusal to follow convention. He also had a following of young men who were opposed to democracy. Some of them later became major figures among the Thirty Tyrants—the corrupt rulers put in place by the Spartans after they defeated Athens. But no one could directly accuse Socrates of supporting the Thirty, and in fact, he had openly disobeyed them. Still, Socrates was perceived to be a bad influence on Athenian youth.

In 399 B.C.E., Socrates was tried by a jury of about 500 men. Slightly more than half voted to convict him of rejecting the Greek religion and harming the city's youth with his teachings. He chose execution rather than admit wrongdoing and go into exile. He then drank poison hemlock, which was commonly used for suicide at the time.

Socrates and his students, particularly Plato, opposed the Sophists and their methods of argument. Like his teacher, Plato sought the virtuous and the ideal. His earlier writings were in the form of dialogues that often featured Socrates as one of the speakers and explained much of what Socrates taught.

Plato also developed his own ideas. He believed that for every real, physical thing that existed, there was a corresponding form that was the ideal of that thing. He said the ideal form existed even if the real thing did not. For example, the form of a chair was separate from the real chairs that people sat on, although the real chairs had qualities of the form.

Forms could also apply to human traits, such as virtue. He said a person could have attributes of the form of virtue, but they could never be completely virtuous. If this sounds a little strange, it did to the ancient Athenians as well.

Plato also wrote about politics and society. His book *Republic* contained many suggestions on how to achieve the ideal political state. It discussed not just government but also education and religion.

Plato disliked traditional Athenian democracy, because he believed most people lacked the intelligence and moral character to rule wisely. He thought "philosopher kings" should rule, educating others in the right way to behave for the good of all society. Plato wrote in his *Republic*, "The law is not concerned with the special happiness of any class in the state, but in trying to produce this condition in the city as a whole, harmonizing and adapting the citizens to one another by persuasion and compulsion. . . ." (quoted in Norman Cantor and Peter L. Klein's *Ancient Thought: Plato and Aristotle*).

ARISTOTLE

Aristotle was Plato's most brilliant student. Aristotle arrived at Athens at age 17 from his home in northern Greece to study with Plato. Aristotle's interests were vast. He not only continued the philosophical discussion of virtue and ethics that he learned from Plato, but also conducted groundbreaking research in the natural sciences.

Aristotle is also considered the first philosopher of science, because he tried to separate philosophy, which is the study of ideas, from science, the study of the natural world. He was the first person to try to spell out what science is and how it should be conducted. He was the first person to talk about biology, the study of life, and then break it down further into zoology, the study of animals. He also created the idea of a formal study of the operations of the polis, leading to the discipline we call politics or political science. (The word *politics* comes from the Greek *politika*, which means "things of the polis"—that is, doing government.)

Aristotle separated mathematics from the study of the physical world—two disciplines that had previously been joined. (The word mathematics comes from the Greek word *mathematikos*, meaning "disposed to learn"; a *mathema* is a lesson or learning.) He then further divided math into arithmetic, plane geometry (the study of two-dimensional shapes) and solid geometry (the study of three-dimensional shapes).

Even within philosophy, Aristotle narrowed down specific categories. He coined the term *metaphysics*, which is the branch of philosophy concerned with what is truly real and the nature of being. Metaphysics is still studied today, and *metaphysical* sometimes has a broader meaning, referring to things that are supernatural or beyond a person's usual perception of reality.

Aristotle was also the founder of a branch of philosophy called *logic*. In a broad sense, logic is the rational thought humans use to solve problems. Aristotle developed rules of logic and logical argument. He created the syllogism, which sets up a thought with three statements. Once the first idea is accepted as true, ideas that are related to it can be shown to be true or false. The classic example is, "All men are mortal. Greeks are men; therefore, all Greeks are mortal." The first two statements are true, so the conclusion must also be true.

Aristotle tried to find a way to bring together observations, common sense and abstract thought. He concerned himself with establishing principles—basic truths. He wrote in *The Physics* (quoted in *Ancient Thought: Plato and Aristotle*) "[I]n the study of nature . . . our first object must be to establish principles." Only by knowing the principles and causes of the natural world could humans truly understand it.

One of the most influential thinkers in history, Aristotle's ideas continue to affect Western culture. Aristotle is also considered the first philosopher of science, because he tried to separate philosophy, which is the study of ideas, from science, the study of the natural world.

MATHEMATICS

Many thinkers whose names are not remembered today created theorems (formulas or statements in mathematics or logic that are proven based on other formulas or statements) to explain the rules of geometry. These theorems rested on proofs that followed logical arguments. Some time around 300 B.C.E., the mathematician Euclid (ca. 325–ca. 265 B.C.E.) took the existing proofs and theorems and collected them into one set that became the foundation of geometry for the next 2,000 years.

Euclid's most famous work is *The Elements*. Plane geometry (the geometry of flat surfaces) and solid geometry (the geometry of three-dimensional shapes), taken together, are still called Euclidean geometry. Another kind of geometry that deals with curved surfaces is called non-Euclidean geometry.

Greek Numerals

Archimedes and other Greek thinkers did not use numerals as they are used today. Like the Romans, Greeks used symbols to represent numbers. Just as each city-state had its own customs, often they also had their own number systems. Modern numerals did not reach Europe until they were brought from India by Arab traders hundreds of years later.

Another great Greek scientist and mathematician of the Hellenistic period was Archimedes (ca. 287–212 B.C.E.). Levers had long been used to lift heavy objects. Archimedes took it upon himself to create a mathematical explanation for how long a lever must be to make it easier to lift a given weight.

Archimedes also gave the first theoretical explanation of pi, the number that begins with 3.14 and continues forever. Pi is the ratio of a circle's circumference (the outer edge) to its diameter (a line from the center point to the outer edge). Pi is part of the formula used to calculate the circumference and area of a circle. In math, it is still indicated by the Greek letter π.

Archimedes was also an active inventor. In this way, he was unlike most Greek scientists, who preferred to deal with abstract ideas. Archimedes is thought to be the inventor of a large screw that bears his name. Turning the screw moves a fluid from a low spot to a higher one. The Archimedes screw is still widely used today in industrial and engineering applications, including grain elevators, sewage treatment plants, and any place where drainage and pumping are required.

Other scientists of the age were very forward thinking. Aristarchus (ca. 310–ca. 230 B.C.E.) was the first to suggest that the sun is at the center of the solar system. The mathematician Eratosthenes (276–194 B.C.E.) was able to calculate the circumference of the Earth to within just 100 kilometers of what we know it is today. Their ideas, however, did not catch on. It would be another 1,700 years or so before their theories were proven correct.

GREEK MEDICINE

Traditionally, the Greeks were like many ancient people. They discovered herbal cures and blended them with superstitions about sickness coming from evil spirits or the gods. The Greek doctor Hippocrates (ca. 460–ca. 337 B.C.E.) was the first person to try to make medicine a true science. (Historians say that the writings attributed to him may have come from more than one source, however. Charles Freeman, in his book *The Greek Achievement,* refers to the "Hippocratic doctors," rather than one person of that name.)

By Hippocrates' time, doctors were already rejecting the idea that magic or other supernatural forces could cause or cure illness. Hippocrates then began applying reason and observation to the human body and illness, just as philosophers did with the universe as a whole.

Some of his conclusions were wrong, such as the notion that four fluids, called humors, controlled human health, and that an imbalance of the humors caused disease. But Hippocrates and his followers did get some things right. They believed that good diet and exercise were the keys to health, and that in many cases the body could heal itself without the need for drugs.

One of Hippocrates' lasting contributions to medicine is known today as the Hippocratic Oath. All doctors after Hippocrates swore to Apollo and the other gods that they would not harm their patients. The basic idea of the oath is still relevant today. Doctors swear to treat the sick to the best of their ability, preserve patient privacy, teach the secrets of medicine to the next generation, and act with compassion.

The Greek scientist Herophilus (ca. 335–280 B.C.E.) added to the understanding of the human body by dissecting corpses. He showed for the first time that the veins and arteries carried blood through the body. He realized that a pulse was connected to a person's heart beat and that the speed of the heart beat could change depending on a person's health. Herophilus was also the first person to detect nerves and discover that they connected to the brain. He has been called the founder of anatomy, the study of the structure of the human body.

CONNECTIONS

A Scientist's Sayings

Along with his scientific contributions, Archimedes is known today for popularizing two phrases. He supposedly ran out of his house—from the bath—after figuring out a scientific problem, shouting the word *eureka* ("I have found it!"). Today, eureka can be used when making any important discovery. It is also the motto of the state of California, referring to the discovery of gold there in 1848.

Archimedes also said, regarding his study of levers, "Give me a place to stand and with a lever I will move the whole world" (quoted in *Bartlett's Familiar Quotations*). Since that time, a wide range of writers and speakers—from President Thomas Jefferson to former vice president Al Gore—have referred to Archimedes' idea that with the right tools and knowledge, one can accomplish the seemingly impossible.

EPILOGUE

ALTHOUGH THE ROMAN EMPIRE DEFEATED THE GREEK city-states in the second century B.C.E., Greek culture had already conquered the Roman Empire. The two civilizations had been having contact since the eighth century B.C.E., when the first Greek colony was founded on Italy's west coast. When Greek cities in Greece itself, Asia Minor, and the Middle East came under Roman dominance, they kept their Greek language and culture. Roman political control was placed on top of a Hellenized society (a society that had adopted Greek culture).

CULTURE CONQUERS THE CONQUERORS

The Romans had mixed feelings about their conquered neighbors. On the one hand, they eagerly took advantage of Greek contributions in arts and science and borrowed heavily from Greek mythology. Athens and the Hellenized Egyptian city of Alexandria remained centers of higher education, and most educated people spoke Greek.

The first Roman emperor, Augustus (63 B.C.E.–14 C.E.), wrote his autobiography in Greek. The Romans absorbed many Greek words into their own language, Latin. However, educated Greek speakers such as Augustus tried not to publicly display too much admiration for Greece. The Romans felt pride in their own accomplishments, and some Romans considered the Greeks to be immoral and inferior.

Romans might have tried to hide how Hellenized they became. But the truth is that they helped spread Greek culture to new parts of the world. At its peak, the Roman Empire stretched from Great Britain to

Saving Sculpture

Modern art lovers are fortunate that the Romans admired their Greek lands and culture, because the Romans helped preserved the Greek artistic tradition (though they did so mostly by stealing them from captured Greek cities). Much of the Greeks' free-standing sculpture was cast in bronze, most of which did not last. Roman artists made copies of these works in marble, and many of them still exist today.

the Middle East, from North Africa to Germany. The Romans did not conquer as much territory as Alexander had, but their control lasted much longer. Their culture became the dominant culture of all their vast empire. And that culture combined the best that both Rome and Classical Greece had to offer. Today, this combination is known as Greco-Roman culture.

In Roman society, Greeks held a number of important jobs, although they often did these jobs as slaves. The Greeks dominated medicine, thanks to the early influence of Hippocrates and his followers. After Hippocrates, the most important doctor of the Greco-Roman world was Galen (129–ca. 200 C.E.). He was born in the Greek city of Pergamum, and came to Rome around 164 C.E. Galen proved, among other things, that urine flows from the kidneys, and he wrote the first major book on anatomy. For centuries, doctors in Europe and the Middle East considered him their most influential source.

Ptolemy (ca. 90–ca. 168 C.E.) was a famous Greek mathematician and astronomer. He wrote a book that argued that the sun and planets revolve around Earth. He was wrong, but his idea was accepted for almost 1,500 years.

EARLY CHRISTIANITY AND THE GREEKS

Greek culture particularly took hold in the eastern parts of the Roman Empire. This was an area where the Greeks had carried out extensive trade and that Alexander had conquered. By the first century C.E., Rome had political control over the Jewish land of Judaea, located in what is now Israel and Jordan.

In this Jewish land, influenced by Romans and Greeks, a new monotheistic (belief in one god) religion emerged: Christianity. Jesus Christ spoke the Middle Eastern language of Aramaic. But the followers who spread his teachings wrote and spoke primarily in Greek, which was the common language of the eastern Roman Empire.

Romans generally tolerated early Christians, although there were sometimes persecutions. In 313 C.E., the Roman emperor Constantine issued an edict, or empire-wide rule, of religious freedom that allowed Christians to worship openly. By 400 C.E., Christianity had become the official religion of the empire.

Later, debates about Christianity and what it meant took place in Greek. These debates reflected the kind of issues ancient Greek philosophers addressed, such as the nature of matter and spirit. Western civilization today might be said to have drawn on two major traditions of thought: Greco-Roman and Judeo-Christian.

By 395 C.E., the Roman Empire had split in half, reunited, and then split again. The eastern portion, including Greece, was ruled from Constantinople (today's Istanbul). Even before this time, though, the Greek-speaking east had become the economic and political center of the Roman Empire. Four of the five bishops of the Christian Church were based in the eastern cities of Constantinople, Alexandria, Jerusalem, and Antioch (in Syria).

Rome itself and the western half of the empire fell to invaders in 476 C.E. The greatness that had been Rome lived on in the more Hellenized east, which became known as the Byzantine Empire.

The Byzantine emperors were aware that they carried on two great cultural traditions. Rome had been famous for its highly developed system of laws and courts, as well as efficient government and skilled engineering. The Byzantines also knew their roots went back even further, to the greatness of Classical Greece and its art, science, and philosophy. Greek scholars in the Byzantine Empire kept that intellectual tradition alive. Western Europe entered into its own Dark Age, when wars continued to break out and only a handful of Christian monks knew the basics of reading and writing.

THE RISE OF ISLAM

During the centuries of the Dark Ages in Western Europe, ancient Greek culture was absorbed by another people: the Arabs. In the seventh century, Muhammad (ca. 570–632), a merchant from Arabia (now Saudi Arabia), founded a new religion called Islam.

Muhammad and his followers set out on wars of conquest. Soon the Islamic Arabs dominated the Middle East, North Africa, and part of Spain. Their lands included parts of what had been the old Greek, Persian, and Roman Empires. These invaders were sometimes welcomed by native Greeks as being less harmful than earlier Byzantine conquerors.

Through their expansion, the Arabs and the people they ruled came into contact with the Byzantine Empire. Islamic scholars began to translate works by Aristotle, Plato, and other Greeks into Arabic. The scholars also read Greek texts on medicine, science, and math, then combined what they learned with ideas from Iran and India.

From the 700s through the 1200s, the Arabs battled Western kingdoms that arose from the remains of Rome's empire. The Arabs also

Importance of Logos

Dialogues were at the heart of Plato's writing. At the heart of the word *dialogue* is the Greek word *logos*. In a general sense, *logos* means "word" or "speech." The prefix *dia* means "through," "apart," or "across," so a dialogue features words sent across from one person to another. To the ancient Greeks, *logos* also had a deeper meaning: the reason or order that controls the universe. Early Christian writers used *logos* to mean the literal word of Jesus Christ, as well as the order and wisdom he represented for the universe. *Logos* is still used that way today.

Seeking Truth

An early Islamic philosopher, al-Kindi (ca. 801–866), expressed the Arabs' enthusiasm for knowledge coming from the Greeks. He wrote (as cited by Albert Hourani in *A History of the Arab Peoples*), "We should not be ashamed to acknowledge truth from whatever source it comes to us, even if it is brought to us by former generations and foreign peoples." Then he echoed the values of Socrates and Aristotle by adding, "For him who seeks the truth there is nothing of higher value than truth itself."

clashed with the Byzantine Empire. Yet the despite their conflicts with the descendants of Greece and Rome, the Arabs played a key role in the development of modern Western culture.

Latin scholars in Western Europe knew that the Arabs had access to works that had been lost in the West. Both Arabic translations of ancient Greek works and original Arabic studies influenced by the Greeks were eventually translated into Latin. At the time, Latin was the language all educated people spoke in Western Europe. Western scholars finally had a chance to discover the wisdom of ancient Greece.

THE OTTOMANS AND INDEPENDENCE

The Arabs did not conquer the Byzantine Empire. But another Islamic people, the Ottoman Turks, did. The Turks came out of Central Asia and settled in Asia Minor. Under their ruler Osman I (1259–1324), they slowly began taking over Byzantine territory. By the mid-15th century, the Turks' rule extended into the Balkans. In 1453 they captured Constantinople, ending the Byzantine Empire.

The Turks renamed the city Istanbul and made it the capital of their Ottoman Empire. After their victory, they looted the city. In the process, they destroyed many Greek documents, including the only surviving copies of ancient Greek works, such as plays by Euripides.

Once again, the Greeks were under foreign control. They would remain part of this new Islamic Ottoman Empire for almost 400 years. The Turks, however, let the Greeks practice Christianity, and a class of educated Greeks served in the Ottoman government. Greeks also played an important role as traders, and Greek priests and monks had ties with Orthodox Christian leaders across Eastern Europe.

Educated Greeks in the Turkish Empire kept alive the memory of ancient Greece. They also led the calls for independence. Many Europeans, who had rediscovered Classical Greek literature and philosophy, saw how important Greece had been in shaping Western culture. Some writers and intellectuals believed the people who had given the world so much should once again have their own nation.

In 1821, a group of Greeks rebelled against the Ottoman Empire. That revolution failed. But by 1830, with help from other European nations, Greece became an independent nation—this time a unified one. Two years later, the Greeks crowned a Bavarian prince, Otto, as

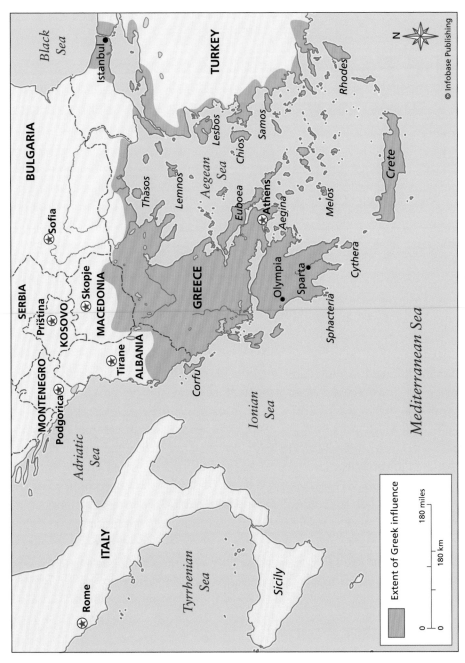

Greek influence in antiquity stretched from the western coastal areas of modern Turkey to southern Macedonia and Albania, including all of modern Greece.

The Parthenon Marbles Controversy

As in ancient times, the Parthenon still stands on a hill overlooking all of Athens. But it has gone through several transformations. After serving Greeks as a temple to Athena, it was used as a Christian church, and then as a mosque (a Muslim house of worship) during the Ottoman Empire.

The Parthenon was badly damaged in the late 1600s, when the Italian city-state of Venice controlled some of the Greek islands in the Ionian Sea and attacked mainland Greece. The Turks used the Parthenon to store munitions, which exploded during the Venetian attack. The Parthenon was left in ruins. It was further altered in the early 1800s, when British diplomat and art collector Thomas Bruce, Lord Elgin (1766–1841) removed the sculptured friezes from around the building.

In 1816, the British Museum in London purchased much of what was then called the Elgin Marbles from Elgin. He claimed he had taken them out of Greece to preserve them from further ruin. Some British writers, however, said that taking the sculptures ruined what was left of the Parthenon. They added that no one had a right to steal art, especially pieces that represented such as strong cultural legacy, no matter what reasons they gave for doing so.

After World War II, some people suggested the British should give back the marbles to thank the Greeks for their resistance against Nazi Germany. The British government refused.

Interest in the issue was renewed in 1982 when Greek actress Melina Mercouri, who was then the Greek minister of culture, addressed the International Conference of Ministers of Culture in Mexico. She pleaded for the friezes to be returned to Athens.

---

their first king. They hoped his connections would help bind the new country to the more established nations of Europe.

GREECE TODAY

As an independent nation, Greece has gone through difficult times. Internal struggles led to several changes in kingship. The country was caught up in various Balkan wars and World War I. During World War II, Nazi Germany occupied Greece. After the Germans were driven out

Sculptures that form part of the Parthenon Marbles are now on display at the British Museum in London. There is an international movement to return them to Greece, but so far the British Museum says it will not give them up.

A committee of British classics scholars was formed in 1983 to lobby for return of the sculptures, now known as the Parthenon Marbles, to Greece. In 2000, the Greek government proposed to the British House of Commons that the location of the Parthenon Marbles was more important than actual ownership. Should they not be as close to their original setting as possible?

Still, some people argued that keeping the marbles in a British museum protects them from the high levels of air pollution in Athens. Besides, some officials claimed, Elgin did not steal the marbles; he had permission from the ruling Ottoman Turks to take the statues, and he paid for them.

Today, a new Acropolis Museum is planned to protect and preserve all of the Parthenon's sculptures, including the Parthenon Marbles. The viewpoint of the British Committee for the Restitution of the Parthenon Marbles, according to their Web site, is that "It is inconceivable that over half of its [the Parthenon's] celebrated sculptural elements should be exhibited 2,000 miles away from the . . . actual monument for which they were expressly designed and carved." So far, the British Museum's reply is that the marbles are staying in London.

in 1944, a civil war followed. On one side were those who were against the Greek monarchy and supported communism, a political system marked by one-party rule and government ownership of all property and businesses. Their opponents supported Western-style democracy (and the Greek monarchy), and private ownership of property. The struggle was violent and bitter.

The democratic forces eventually won, and in 1949 the Greeks established a government with both a king and elected lawmakers. During the 1960s this government was replaced by a military dictatorship.

This lasted until 1974, when the dictatorship collapsed. The next year, the Greeks wrote a new constitution that established a republic, ending the role of the monarchy.

Today Greece is a member of the European Union and the North Atlantic Treaty Organization (NATO). The economy still features elements of its ancient past. For example, the Greeks have the world's largest fleet of merchant ships. And Greek farmers still raise grain and olives, just as they have for thousands of years. Yet the Greeks are also building a modern nation, putting more emphasis on telecommunications and industry. Perhaps most important to the economy is tourism, as people from around the world come to explore one of the historic hearts of Western civilization.

THE LEGACY OF ANCIENT GREECE

This book has detailed many of the gifts passed down to modern times from the Greeks: the words and concepts they used that are still common today; lasting works of art and mythological tales that inspire new generations; systems of thought that are still taught in schools. Equally important is the Greek spirit that questioned why the world and its people are the way they are. The ancient Greeks encouraged original thought in seeking answers, rather than merely accepting what others said.

That spirit of openly asking questions and exploring the answers lives on in many forms, thanks to the Greek writings that have endured for more than 2,500 years. The great writings of Aristotle and others "laid the foundations of Western learning . . . from literature to astronomy, from medicine to historiography," according to Paul Cartledge in *The Cambridge Illustrated History of Ancient Greece.*

Part of that vast body of knowledge was lost to Western Europe during the Dark Ages, but the best of Athens and Rome slowly reemerged and spread to a wider audience than ever before. That reemergence rested on two developments, one technical and one intellectual.

In the 15th century, German goldsmith Johannes Gutenberg (ca. 1400–ca. 1467) invented a printing press that used movable type, bringing publishing to Europe. For the first time, people could buy books, and printers created the first copies of ancient texts for European audiences. The fact that books became more widely available created a desire among people to read in their own language. Ancient Greek writings were translated and published in books. They reached a wider audience than any of the classic authors could have dreamed possible.

The intellectual trend that created an interest in the classics was the Renaissance. During the 14th century, Italy was dominated by powerful city-states—just as in ancient Greece. The Italian city-states had thriving economies, and wealthy families gave money to artists and scholars. These creative minds began to explore the classic works of Greece and Rome for inspiration. They turned away from the Christian culture that had dominated the arts and education since the fall of the Roman Empire in the West.

This Renaissance (Italian for "rebirth") led to paintings, sculpture, and architecture that were based on Greek models. Artists also felt free to show scenes from Greek mythology and contemporary everyday life, as the ancients had, instead of showing only Christian themes.

In education, scholars read Plato, Aristotle, and the other Greeks and debated their ideas. They found that many of their ancient conclusions were still relevant. Petrarch (1304–1374), an Italian poet, played a key role in this revival. He was considered the first modern humanist—someone who places the study of human concerns above religion, just as the Greek philosophers had done centuries before. Petrarch tried to learn ancient Greek, and he encouraged other scholars to do the same. They took his advice, and for the next few hundred years educated people across Europe learned ancient Greek so they could study the classics as they were written.

The rise of humanism led to a new interest in science. Earlier scientists had already been influenced by Greek works that had been translated into Latin. The scientific method of the Greeks, based on reasoning and observation,

CONNECTIONS

Greek Moons

In 1610, using a telescope of his own design, Italian astronomer Galileo Galilei discovered four moons circling the planet Jupiter. Astronomers have since found dozens more orbiting that large planet and have given them names taken from Greek mythology. The first moons Galileo saw were named for three women who had relationships with Zeus (Jupiter is his Roman name): Io, Callisto, and Europa. The fourth, Ganymede, was named for a young Trojan man whom Zeus brought to Olympus to serve the gods.

The word *planet* has Greek roots. It comes from the word *planes,* meaning "wanderer." This reflects what the ancient Greeks realized—that the planets did not follow an orderly, circular path through the sky. Modern scientists showed the Greeks were right: The planets orbit in a changing path, not a perfect circle.

The founders of the U.S. government admired the ancient Greeks' commitment to democracy. The freedoms protected in the American Bill of Rights, shown here, are some of the same ones the Greeks cherished—freedom of speech, freedom of religion, and the right to have a jury trial.

was expanded to include experimentation. Scientists came up with a theory, based on existing knowledge, and then tested it to see if it was true.

The scientific revolution that began in the 16th century drew upon the spirit of open inquiry that came from the Greeks. These new scientists sometimes discovered things that proved some Greek concepts to be wrong. Ptolemy's old system for explaining the universe, for example, did not survive. Polish scientist Nicholas Copernicus (1473–1543) suggested and Italian astronomer Galileo Galilei (1564–1642) proved that the sun was the center of our solar system, not the Earth. Galileo, however, did not have the same freedom as ancient Greek scientists. The Roman Catholic Church forced the Italian astronomer to declare he was wrong, even though he knew he was right.

European settlers who came to North America brought their knowledge of Classical Greece and Rome with them. When American revolutionaries considered various forms of government, they held up Classical Rome as an ideal. In the 18th century, most Americans did not want a direct democracy, as in the Athens of Pericles. They preferred a republic, as the Romans had, with men (and only men) who owned property electing others to create their laws. Still, many American and British thinkers admired features of the Greek political system.

Aristotle wrote extensively about the constitution of Athens, and Americans such as Samuel Adams (1722–1803) saw that Great Britain had its own unwritten constitution that included laws dating back to the 13th century. That document placed limits on the king's power. Americans also saw that the British government featured three elements Aristotle had discussed: monarchy, aristocracy, and democracy (though not direct democracy).

The men who governed after the American Revolution favored eliminating monarchy and limiting the aristocracy. They wanted to give the people—the *demos*—a greater role in the government. The U.S. leaders went one step further than the British and wrote a formal constitution. It described exactly what the government would include and how it would function. The Americans also created a Bill of Rights, spelling out individual freedoms that would be protected. These freedoms included some of the same ones the Greeks cherished—freedom of speech, freedom of religion, and the right to have a jury trial.

TIME LINE

1200s B.C.E.	Mycenaean culture reaches its high point. Troy is destroyed.
1100 B.C.E.	Struggles among Mediterranean cultures bring a Dark Age in the entire region. Mycenaean palaces are destroyed.
776 B.C.E.	As Greek civilization rebounds, the first Olympic games are held in Olympia.
750–700 B.C.E.	The Greek alphabet is developed. Homer's poetry is first written down.
750-550 B.C.E.	Greek colonization means new Greek city-states are formed throughout the Mediterranean and Black Sea areas.
630 B.C.E.	Sparta enslaves the defeated Messenians, who will serve as agricultural slaves for Sparta until they are freed by Thebes in the fourth century B.C.E.
600 B.C.E.	Hoplite infantry becomes common throughout Greece. Sappho writes poetry about the personal experience of love and longing.
594 B.C.E.	Solon reforms Athenian law and extends power to the lower classes.
ca. 585–550 B.C.E.	The earliest Greek philosophers, Thales, Anaximander, and Anaximemes, present new ideas about the universe that have nothing to do with the gods.
508 B.C.E.	Cleisthenes puts Athens on clear path to democracy.
490 B.C.E.	Though greatly outnumbered, hoplites from Athens and Plataea defeat the army of the Persian Empire at Marathon to win the first Persian War.
480–479 B.C.E.	Greek victories in the second Persian War usher in the Athenian empire and the Classical period of Greek civilization, with enormous achievements in government, literature, drama, architecture, and art.
447–432 B.C.E.	The Parthenon is built in Athens.
431–404 B.C.E.	The Peloponnesian War is fought between Athens and Sparta and their allies.
399 B.C.E.	Athenian philosopher and teacher Socrates is executed.
370 B.C.E.	Thebes, under the leadership of Epiminondas, invades Sparta and frees the Messenian helots. (Epiminondas dies in a later Theban victory in 362 B.C.E.)
338 B.C.E.	Philip II of Macedon defeats a coalition of Greek forces and establishes the League of Corinth. After Philip's assassination in 336 B.C.E., his son Alexander the Great conquers the Persian Empire and Egypt.
331 B.C.E.	Alexander founds Alexandria in Egypt. It will become the capital of the far-ranging Greek-speaking world after his death.
323 B.C.E.	Alexander dies. Three Hellenistic kingdoms are established by his generals.
146 B.C.E.	The Roman Empire conquers Greece and Macedonia.

GLOSSARY

agora   open-air marketplace

allies   countries or groups that work together, especially during wartime; their unity is called an *alliance*

archaeologists   scientists who study ancient people by studying the items they left behind

architecture   the way buildings are designed and built

archon   an appointed governor in ancient Athens

aristocracy   a small group of people of the highest class or who have the most money and power; individual members of this group are *aristocrats*

artifacts   items from daily life left behind by a group of people

battering ram   a heavy object swung or rammed against a door to break it down

cavalry   soldiers who fight on horseback

chariot   a cart with two wheels that is pulled by horses

city-state   a city and its surrounding farms that functions as a separate nation

civil   relating to the citizens and the things that concern them

colony   an area that is under the political control of another country and is occupied by settlers from that country

commerce   the activity of buying and selling

coup   quick, violent takeover of a government

deme   a village or district in Athens; the *demes* were based on family ties and were the basic political unit of Athens

descendants   relatives who trace their roots back to one person

epic   a long poem about the actions and adventures of heroic or legendary figures or about the history of a nation

fertility   the ability to easily grow (for plants) or have offspring (for animals and people)

Hellas   the word the Greeks used to mean the entire Greek world; what Greeks today call their nation

Hellenism   Greek culture; the adjective is *Hellenistic*

Hellenized   having adopted Greek culture

helot   a serf in ancient Sparta, intermediate in status between slaves and citizens

hoplite   a heavily armed foot soldier

infantry   soldiers who fight on foot

logic   the study of the rules and tests of sound reasoning

mercenary   a foreign soldier hired to fight for another country

metic   free person who was a citizen of a different city-state or from a foreign country; *metics* could not participate in the Athenian democracy

monarchy   a government controlled by a king

myth   a traditional story, usually involving gods or magic, that often helps explain historical events or a particular custom, belief, or aspect of nature

oligarchy   a government ruled by a council of aristocrats

omen   a sign that predicts the future

oracle   a priest or priestess who is said to be able to communicate with the gods and deliver messages from them

orator   an especially skilled public speaker

peninsula   an area of land surrounded by water on three sides

phalanx   a group of soldiers standing and moving in very close formation

philosopher   a person who thinks about the meaning of life and how to lead a better life; in ancient times, many philosophers were also scientists

philosophy   the study of the nature of the world

plague   a highly contagious disease that spreads rapidly and kills many people

polis   a Greek city-state

Renaissance   a period in history, beginning in the 13th century, that stressed the importance of education, art, and the worth of the individual; it was also marked by a rediscovery of ancient Greek and Roman culture

republic   a government in which voters elect lawmakers, who represent the interests of the people

rhetoric   the art of speaking or writing effectively

ritual   a ceremony carried out according to religious laws and customs

satire   comedy that critiques politics, government, or society in a humorous way

serf   an agricultural worker who must work for a single master who owns the land

siege   cutting off a town or fort from the outside so it cannot receive supplies and the inhabitants cannot escape

successor   a person who comes after another and inherits or continues in the offices they held

tactic   an action or strategy that is carefully planned to achieve a specific result

terracing   building a number of flat platforms, usually into the side of a hill; *terrace farming* is farming the land that is on these flat platforms

theorem   a formula or statement in mathematics or logic that is proven based on other formulas or statements

trireme   a long, narrow Athenian warship powered by three rows of oarsmen

tyrant   a person who uses their power in a cruel and unreasonable way

BIBLIOGRAPHY

Adkins, Lesley, and Roy A. Adkins, *Handbook to Life in Ancient Rome, Updated Edition*. New York: Facts On File, 2004.

Aesop's Fables. Translated by George Fyler Townsend. Available online. The Internet Classics Archive. URL: http://classics.mit.edu/Aesop/fab.html. Accessed April 29, 2008.

Aristophanes, *Four Comedies*, Translated by Dudley Fitts. New York: Harcourt, Brace & World, 1962.

Aristotle, *The Politics of Aristotle*, Book 2. Translated by Benjamin Jowett. Available online. "Aristotle: Spartan Women," Ancient History Sourcebook. URL: http://www.fordham.edu/halsall/ancient/aristotle-spartanwomen.html. Accessed March 30, 2008.

Atchity, Kenneth J., editor, *The Classical Greek Reader*. New York: Henry Holt and Company, 1996.

Boardman, John, Jasper Griffin, and Oswyn Murray, *The Oxford History of Greece and the Hellenistic World*. Oxford, U.K.: Oxford University Press, 1988.

Cahill, Thomas, *Sailing the Wine-Dark Sea: Why the Greeks Matter*. New York: Nan A. Talese/Doubleday, 2003.

Camp, John, and Elizabeth Fisher, *The World of the Ancient Greeks*. New York: Thames & Hudson, 2002.

Cantor, Norman, editor, *The Encyclopedia of the Middle Ages*. New York: Viking, 1999.

Cantor, Norman, and Peter L. Klein, editors, *Ancient Thought: Plato and Aristotle*. Waltham, Mass.: Blaisdell Publishing, 1969.

Cartledge, Paul, editor, *The Cambridge Illustrated History of Ancient Greece*. Cambridge, U.K.: Cambridge University Press, 1998.

"The Case for the Return." British Committee for the Restitution of the Parthenon Marbles. Available online. URL: http://www.parthenonuk.com/the_case_for_the_return.php. Accessed July 28, 2004.

Dewald, Carolyn, and John Marincola, *The Cambridge Companion to Herodotus*. Cambridge, U.K.: Cambridge University Press, 2006.

Drabble, Margaret, editor, *The Oxford Companion to English Literature*, Revised ed. Oxford, U.K.: Oxford University Press, 1995.

Durant, Will, *The Life of Greece*. New York: Simon and Schuster, 1939.

Fine, John V. A., *The Ancient Greeks: A Critical History*. Cambridge, Mass.: Belknap Press,1983.

Finley, M. I., *The Ancient Greeks*. New York: Viking Penguin, Inc. 1971.

——, *Economy and Society in Ancient Greece*. New York: Viking Press, 1981.

Flaceliere, Robert, *Daily Life in Greece at the Time of Pericles*. London: Phoenix Press, 1965.

Freeman, Charles, *The Greek Achievement: The Foundation of the Western World*. New York: Penguin Books, 1999.

Gardner, Helen, *Art Through the Ages*, Revised edition. New York: Harcourt Brace Jovanovich, 1975.

Garraty John A., and Peter Gay, editors, *The Columbia History of the World*. New York: Harper & Row, 1972.

Geanakoplos, Deno J., *Medieval Western Civilization and the Byzantine and Islamic World*. Lexington, Ky.: D.C. Heath and Company, 1979.

Grant, Michael, *The Founders of the Western World: A History of Greece and Rome*. New York: Charles Scribner's Sons, 1991.

Hamilton, Edith, *Mythology*. New York: Warner Books, 1942, 1969.

Hanson, Victor Davis, *The Wars of the Ancient Greeks*. New York: Sterling Publishing, 1999.

Harris, Nathaniel, *History of Ancient Greece*. New York: Barnes & Noble Books, 2000.

Herodotus, *The Histories*. Translated by Aubery de Selincourt. London: Penguin Classics, 2003.

———, *The Histories*, Translated by Robin Waterfield. Oxford, U.K.: Oxford University Press, 1998.

"Herodotus: Solon and Croesus," Ancient History Sourcebook. Available online. URL: http://www.fordham.edu/halsall/ancient/herodotus-creususandsolon.html. Accessed July 10, 2004.

Hesiod, *Theogony and Works and Days.* Translated by Catherine Schlegel and Henry Weinfield. Ann Arbor, Mich.: University of Michigan Press, 2006.

———, "Works and Days." Available online. The Online Classical and Medieval Library. URL: http://sunsite.berkeley.edu/OMACL/Hesiod/works.html. Accessed July 24, 2004.

Homer, *The Illiad*, Translated by Robert Fagles. New York: Penguin Group, 1990.

———, *The Odyssey*, Translated by Robert Fagles. New York: Penguin Group, 1996.

Honderich, Ted, editor, *The Oxford Companion to Philosophy*. Oxford, U.K.: Oxford University Press, 1995.

Hopper, R. J., *The Early Greeks*. New York: Harper & Row, 1976.

Hourani, Albert, *A History of the Arab Peoples*. Cambridge, Mass.: Belknap Press, 1991.

James, Peter, and Nick Thorpe, *Ancient Inventions*. New York: Ballantine Books, 1994.

Kaplan, Justin, editor, *Bartlett's Familiar Quotations*, 16th ed. Boston: Little, Brown and Company, 1992.

Long, Roderick T., "The Athenian Constitution." LewRockwell.com. Available online. URL: http://www.lewrockwell.com/long/long8.html. Accessed July 20, 2004.

Macrone, Michael, *By Jove!: Brush Up Your Mythology*. New York: Cader Books, 1992.

Martin, Thomas R., *Ancient Greece: From Prehistoric to Hellenistic Times*. New Haven, Conn.: Yale University Press, 2000.

Merriam-Webster's Geographical Dictionary, 3rd ed. Springfield, Mass.: Merriam-Webster, 1997.

National Public Radio, *All Things Considered* (transcripts), "Athens and Sparta Formalize Peace After 2,000 Years," hosted by Neal Conan, March 12, 1996.

National Public Radio, *Talk of the Nation* (transcripts), "Classical Education," hosted by Neal Conan, June 29, 1998.

"Olive Subsidies Threaten the Mediterranean Environment." WWF-UK. Available online. URL: http://www.wwf-uk.org/News/n_0000000290.asp. Accessed July 15, 2004.

"The Parthenon of Nashville, Tennessee." Metropolitan Government of Nashville and Davidson County. Available online. URL: http://www.nashville.gov/parthenon. Accessed July 15, 2004.

Plato, *The Last Days of Socrates*, Translated by Hugh Tredennick. Middlesex, U.K.: Penguin Books, 1969.

Plato, *Meno*, Translated by Benjamin Jowett. New South Wales, Australia: ReadHowYouWant, 2006.

———, *Symposium*, Translated by Benjamin Jowett. The Internet Classics Archive. Available online. URL: http://classics.mit.edu/Plato/symposium.html. Accessed July 15, 2004.

Plautus, *Three Comedies*, Translated by Erich Segal. New York: Bantam Books, 1969.

Pollitt, J. J., *The Art of Ancient Greece: Sources and Documents*. Cambridge, U.K.: Cambridge University Press, 1990.

Pomeroy, Sarah B., Stanley M. Burstein, Walter Donlan, and Jennifer Tolbert Roberts, *Ancient Greece: A Political, Social, and Cultural History*. New York: Oxford University Press, 1999.

Pritchard, James B., editor, *The Harper Concise Atlas of the Bible*. New York: HarperCollins, 1991.

Quennell, Marjorie, and C. H. B. Quennell, *Everyday Things in Ancient Greece*, Revised by Kathleen Freeman. New York: G. P Putnam's Sons, 1965.

Sage, Michael M., *Warfare in Ancient Greece: A Sourcebook*. Florence, Ky.: Routledge, 1996.

Shelley, Percy Bysshe, "Hellas." Poetry Archive. Available online. URL: http://www.poetry-archive.com/s/hellas.html. Accessed July 20, 2005.

Sophocles, *Antigone*. Translated by Ian Johnston. Arlington, Va.: Richer Resources Publications, 2005.

Strassler, Robert B., editor, *The Landmark Thucydides: A Comprehensive Guide to the Peloponnesian War*. New York: The Free Press, 1996.

Thucydides, *History of the Peloponnesian War*, Translated by Rex Warner. New York: Penguin Books, 1972.

Trichopoulou, Antonia, *et al.*, "Adherence to a Mediterranean Diet and Survival in a Greek Population." *The New England Journal of Medicine*, June 26, 2003, Vol. 348:2599-2608.

Watkin, David, *A History of Western Architecture*, 2nd ed. London: Lawrence King, 1996.

Xenophon, *Anabasis*. Translated by Carleton L. Brownson. Cambridge, Mass: Harvard University Press, 1998.

———, *On the Polity of the Spartans*. "The Spartan War Machine," Ancient History Sourcebook. Available online. URL: http://www.fordham.edu/halsall/ancient/xenophon-spartanwar.html. Accessed April 16, 2008.

Yaman, Ebru, "Music sleuth tracks down harps and lyres of ancients." *The Australian*, April 16, 2003.

Zimmerman, J. E., *Dictionary of Classical Mythology*. New York: Bantam Books, 1964.

FURTHER RESOURCES

BOOKS

Biesty, Stephen, and Stewart Ross, *Greece in Spectacular Cross-section* (Oxford, U.K.: Oxford University Press, 2006)

> The year is 436 B.C.E. and 11-year-old Neleus is taking a trip with his father and brother from his home in Miletus to see the Olympic Games in Olympia. He has many adventures and sees many sights along the way: Athenian warships at the sacred island of Delos, the silver mines of Laurion, the busy port and streets of Athens, and the sacred oracle at Delphi. Each is drawn in amazing detail, with cross-sections, cutaways and explosions. Each drawing is backed up by authoritative text. No aspect of Greek life is left out, including domestic life, religion and the gods, the role of women, children and education, philosophy and learning, myths and legends, government, politics and law, economy and trade, warfare and slavery, the Olympic Games, music and drama, painting, pottery and sculpture, building and architecture, and ships and sailing.

Bordessa, Kris, *Tools of the Ancient Greeks: A Kid's Guide to the History & Science of Life in Ancient Greece* (White River Junction, Vt.: Nomad Press, 2006)

> Discover the origins of ancient Greek ideas about anatomy, geography, and democracy, and the ways they continue to influence thinking today. Profiles of famous historical figures explain how their inventions are used in the modern world and provide insight into how the Greeks thought. There are 15 activities that recreate some of the Greeks' scientific discoveries while learning how to use scientific reasoning, develop basic ideas, and find supporting evidence.

Colum Padraic, *The Children's Homer: The Adventures of Odysseus and the Tale of Troy* (London: Aladdin Children's Books, 2004)

> This is the perfect book for children interested in the stories of the *Illiad* and the *Odyssey*. Using narrative threads from Homer's classics, the author weaves a wonderful adventure tale. He starts when Achilles, aided by the gods, waged war against the Trojans. Then he follows Odysseus on his dangerous journey home.

D'Aulaire, Ingri, and Edgar Parin D'Aulaire, *D'Aulaire's Book of Greek Myths* (New York: Delacorte Press, 1992)

> All the great gods and goddesses of ancient Greece are depicted in this beautifully illustrated book. Read about mighty Zeus, lord of the universe, elegant Athena, goddess of wisdom, powerful Hera, queen of Olympus, and moody Poseidon, ruler of the sea. From petty arguments to heroic deeds, their stories have qualities that are both human and fantastic. This is a wonderful introduction to mythology.

Day, Nancy, *Your Travel Guide to Ancient Greece* (Minneapolis, Minn.: Runestone Press, 2000)

> Imagine a trip to the ancient world with this travel-guide to fifth-century B.C.E. Greece. It describes the cultural influences, climate, cities to visit, monetary system, local customs, food, accommodations, shopping, and more. A short who's who of famous people and some simple activities wrap up this volume. Special topic boxes add related and sometimes funny trivia.

Evslin, Bernard, *Heroes, Gods and Monsters of the Greek Myths* (New York: Laurel Leaf, Reissue edition, 1984)

This compelling book introduces the wondrous and terrifying world of superhuman beings, such as Medusa and the Minotaur, and gods like Zeus, Athena, and Poseidon—brought to life through exciting retellings of great adventures.

Haaren, John H., and A. B. Poland, *Famous Men of Greece* (Chapel Hill, N.C.: Yesterday's Classics, 2006)

Biographical sketches of 35 of the most prominent characters in the history of ancient Greece, from legendary times to its fall in 146 B.C.E. Among the profiles are Jason and the Golden Fleece, Solon, the hero of Marathon, Pericles, Socrates, and more. Each story is told in a clear, straightforward way.

Homer (translated by Robert Fagles), *The Iliad and The Odyssey* (New York: Penguin Classics, 1999)

These well-received translations of Homer's classics are especially readable for modern audiences who want to tackle Homer's original epic stories. These tales of war, heroism, gods, monsters, and returning home again are as compelling now as they were 3,000 years ago.

McAllister, Emma, *The Pocket Timeline of Ancient Greece* (New York: Oxford University Press, 2006)

From the mysterious very ancient origins of the Greeks to the Archaic Period, the Classical Period, the Hellenistic Period and the legacy of Greek civilization, this book sums up Greek history in short sections. Each is illustrated with wonderful photos of Greek art and artifacts.

Pearson, Anne, *Ancient Greece (Eyewitness Books)* (New York: DK Publishing, 2007)

Learn about the history of Greek civilization, politics and power, gods and heroes, festivals and oracles, temples, women, growing up in Greece, fun and games, food and wine, clothes, beauty and wisdom, death and the afterlife, farming and fishing, trade, sports, warfare, and more by looking at Greek art and artifacts and drawings that recreate ancient Greece. The book includes a glossary and a who's who.

Sacks, David, *Encyclopedia of the Ancient Greek World* (New York: Facts On File, 2005)

This readable, lively collection of facts is presented in alphabetical entries that are logical, comprehensive, and cross-indexed. More than 550 entries describe the people, places, & events of more than 2,000 years of Greek civilization. Includes not only poets, politicians, and rulers but also topics relating to the everyday lives of average citizens, women, and slaves. Other topics include history, politics, warfare and weaponry, social organizations, the arts, literature, language, mythology, geography, science and technology, clothing, religion, and more.

Skelton, Debra, and Pamela Dell, *Empire of Alexander the Great* (New York: Chelsea House, 2009)

Learn more about the Hellenistic Age and how Alexander the Great, the Macedonian king, spread Greek civilization throughout the known world. This detailed look at Alexander's empire includes history, culture, religion, art, science, and everyday life.

DVDS

The Greeks: Crucible of Civilization (PBS Paramount, 2005)

This is the DVD of the PBS documentary that tells the story of Greek democracy from its first stirrings in 500 B.C.E. through to the cataclysmic wars that virtually destroyed the empire. It ends with a fascinating look at how the Greeks were defeated, yet their philosophy endured and changed the world forever. Actor Liam Neeson narrates, some critical events are re-created by actors, and computer animation shows what ancient ruins looked like when they were new. The photography at ancient sites is spectacular.

WEB SITES

Ancient Greece
www.ancientgreece.com

This detailed and wonderfully illustrated look at ancient Greece is divided into sections on history, architecture and art, geography, mythology, people, wars, culture and society, and the Olympics. There is also a glossary and a photo gallery of Greek art and artifacts. An extensive resources section is also included. The site is laid out in a way that makes navigation easy.

Ancient Greece
http://greece.mrdonn.org

This site is divided into three sections: Greek origins and history, daily life, and the Greek city-states. The sections on the Greek philosophers are especially well done, and include really clear, easy-to-understand explanations of their ideas. There are also sections with interactive games and a library of clip art about ancient Greece that you can download.

Ancient Greek Literature and Mythology
www.infoplease.com/spot/ancientgreece-litmyth. html

This site from InfoPlease includes translations of plays, poetry, and literature, biographies of important figures, quizzes and games, heroes and legends, and an explanation of the references to Greek stories in the Harry Potter novels.

The Ancient Olympics
www.perseus.tufts.edu/Olympics/

At this site, developed by the Classics department at Tufts University, compare ancient and modern Olympic sports, tour the site of Olympia as it looks today, learn about the social and cultural ideas that are associated with the Games, and understand the Olympic spirit. The site also features stories of real ancient Greek athletes who were famous in their own time. Art from pottery and other sources illustrates their stories.

British Committee for the Restitution of the Parthenon Marbles
www.parthenonuk.com

The committee's official Web site contains detailed information on the Parthenon (Elgin) Marbles, together with the case for their return to Athens. News stories detail conferences that discuss returning artifacts to their countries of origin and point out any new developments regarding the Parthenon Marbles.

Elpenor: Home of the Greek Word
www.ellopos.net/elpenor/

Elpenor is a collection in Greek and English of all periods of Greek literature, including downloadable versions of Plato, Aristotle and the New Testament of the Bible. Language pages feature lessons in ancient Greek, starting with the alphabet, continuing with Homer and combining grammar and syntax with an attempt to understand how these texts are relevant to life today. There is also a section on how Greek ideas have influenced Western thought. The site is illustrated with photographs and period art.

The Greeks
www.pbs.org/empires/thegreeks

This multimedia Web site, a companion to the PBS documentary "The Greeks: Crucible of Civilization," offers a lesson in ancient Greek, enables visitors to download a "virtual Socrates," or explore Athens with an interactive map. There is also a 3-D virtual Parthenon and biographies of many important figures in Greek history. The site includes a time line of Greek history, and information on how the documentary was made.

History for Kids: Ancient Greece
www.historyforkids.org/learn/greeks/index.htm

Learn about all aspects of ancient Greek life, including the economy, language and literature, clothing, philosophy, art, religion, food, sports, government, and more. There is also an arts and crafts section with instructions for hands-on projects. Each article has many links that encourage further exploration.

Spartan World

www. spartan-world.de/index.html

This site is all about Sparta. Read about the kings, hoplites, the Persian Empire and Sparta, Spartan shields and emblems, and the way children were brought up in Sparta. The site includes a map and a timeline.

The World of the Greeks

www.ncl.ac.uk/shefton-museum/greeks/index.html

This site is from the Shefton Museum at the University of Newcastle in Great Britain. Tour the museum's collections of Greek arms and armor, pottery and sculpture. Or learn about how the Greeks lived and what they believed. There are fun quizzes to take after the tour.

Worlds Intertwined: Etruscans, Greeks and Romans

www.museum.upenn.edu/new/worlds_intertwined/main.shtml

This site from the University of Pennsylvania Museum of Archaeology and Anthropology explores daily life, religion and death, art, economics and more. Also available is a virtual tour of an exhibit that explains how the ancient Greek, Roman, and Etruscan cultures intertwined.

PICTURE CREDITS

INDEX

ABOUT THE AUTHOR

JEAN KINNEY WILLIAMS is a free-lance writer who lives in Ohio. She has written many non-fiction books on a variety of history and social studies topics, including *Mormon Faith in America* for Facts On File.

History consultant **JOHN W. I. LEE** is associate professor of history at the University of California at Santa Barbara, specializing in the study of ancient Greece, Greek archaeology, and ancient warfare.